Chinook Winds

Aboriginal Dance Project

The Banff Centre Press

7th Generation Books

Published by The Banff Centre Press and 7th Generation Books
in conjunction with The Aboriginal Arts Program – a partnership
of the Aboriginal Film and Video Art Alliance and The Banff
Centre for the Arts.

Canadian Cataloguing in Publication Data
Main entry under title:
Chinook winds : aboriginal dance project
ISBN 1-896923-02-X
1. Indian dance – Canada.
E98.D2C55 1997 793.3'1'08997071 C97-900360-1

Edited by Heather Elton
Contributing editors: Florene Belmore, Paul Seesequasis
Designed by Jerry Longboat
Interviews transcribed by Gloria Manitopyes
Final page layout and pre-press: Mary Squario

Front cover: Jeff Tabvahtah. Photo Don Lee.
Back cover design inspired by a Plains War Bonnet motif.

Printed and bound in Canada.

The Banff Centre Press
The Banff Centre for the Arts
Box 1020–50
Banff, Alberta T0L 0C0

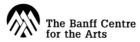

The Banff Centre
for the Arts   7th Generation Books

Chinook Winds

Aboriginal Dance Project

Dancing a Higher Truth
Preface
Jerry P. Longboat

Chinook Winds is born from the awareness that we, as Aboriginal people, have begun to claim our right to stand up and speak our truth. Aboriginal dance is a spiritual expression through which we travel to the ancestral world. Dance is a doorway to powerful wisdom. Its motions express the ancestral memory in our bodies; it is the voice of all our relations.

Aboriginal dance is a true voice, one that rang clear and strong long before we called it a "traditional" voice. It exemplifies oral tradition as story and myth combined into forms of expression through which elders, faithkeepers, healers, and young people speak from their inner selves, their centres.

The elders say we must first own ourselves before we can truly obtain self governance. We must own the bundles that are our languages, songs, stories, art, and dance. In achieving this, our personal and communal circles are completed and our way of living is made harmonious. The power of dance is a significant ingredient in achieving this balance. And, considering the

Jerry Longboat in traditional regalia. Photo Heather Elton.

whole, we must express ourselves as clearly as we can, from deep within all our nations, so that our children, and those yet to come, can share the wisdom and beauty of all our generations.

The *Chinook Winds* project is strongly rooted in Aboriginal cultural principles and oral narratives. By engaging us with songs and music, stories and images, *Chinook Winds* explores connected, unified tribal voices of movement and dance languages. This collaborative dance experience establishes a contemporary expression in the thread of our cultural narrative. It is a place to claim our voice, a manifestation of our will for self determination and original artistic direction. This is rebirth. An act celebrating the depth of our creative voices and the cultural diversity of Aboriginal nations.

In our teachings, knowledge comes from, and is shaped by, the natural world and all its cycles. Therefore, the beginning, or the root, of the culture is the story. In the telling of our personal stories, in whatever language or creative form we use, we are expressing our connection to creation. Through this process we sense and experience the depths of this natural knowledge with the sharing of story. The stories are the very crux of healing. They give voice to the ever-changing connection to all our relations. This legacy lives at the very heart of our collective experience and dance is a primary form of our storytelling. Its variety of forms are an integral aspect in nurturing the health, well-being, and harmony in Aboriginal communities. Dance is an expression of prayer and story, of our relationship to Mother Earth and to one another. It also includes the unspoken records of previous generations, those yet to come, our families, nations, and all creation. In short, it is "in the bones." And, when we dance, our timeless oral narratives possess the ancient stories of wisdom and understanding.

A wise one once said that we must understand that sometimes the questions are more important than the answers. We begin to ask the questions: How do we get there from here? How can we listen, or see, or feel, to find our way to the heart of our truths? How do we learn to trust ourselves to hear the language of the earth?

Chinook Winds addresses these questions and creatively reveals what is alive and present, or, absent and forgotten, around us. These dances contain the innermost cultural stories. There is power in the stories' teachings because they allow for a return to the origin of creation, a mythic time. In doing so, they combine the migratory borders of the mind and the heart into a communal experience. To dance, and then to write about the experiences of these stories, makes the process new again and revisits the creation process.

At no other time in our human journey have we needed more to hear our ancestors' stories than we do now. Those stories, of the relationship our ancestors had with the earth, and the animal, bird, and plant world, are vital in this time of such destruction. Our future depends on our ability to ask the questions, to wait and listen. Finding the pathways to harmonious life with creation is a human responsibility. To rediscover and create vibrant environments for the present is our challenge. To repair and reconnect the circle of our personal and communal power, and to dance from that circle in celebration of our unique gifts as Aboriginal people, is our right. This is the place of self determination. Here lies the source and purpose of *Chinook Winds*.

This place in the creative process marks a point of return. It takes us towards a place of balance, within our centre, our place in the community of all things. It clears our vision and places us in balance with the environment around us. Yet, like any other process, it does not finish there. For the real journey begins after the first few steps are taken. As we take up this new way, our minds and hearts are filled with visions of spirit and the earth that holds us within it. This spirit needs to be nurtured within each of us, and within our nations. Our dances are the gifts and *Chinook Winds* is a vessel for our love of creation.

This book consists of writings and images that tell the story of the Aboriginal Dance Project. It reveals the exciting cultural expression that was *Chinook Winds*. Here, both new and veteran Aboriginal writers, musicians, instructors, and dancers tell their stories through writings, interviews, poetry, and dance. By mapping this collective journey, *Chinook Winds* fulfills an important part of the mandate of the Aboriginal Arts Program at The Banff Centre for the Arts, to further the traditions of oral history and storytelling.

In *Chinook Winds*, we find a place to reclaim our voice, to own ourselves, and to achieve self determination. This original artistic creation is both a rebirth and a celebration of the depth and diversity of our creative voices. In exploring the fusion of modern and traditional dance styles, the past merges with the present to create a new, dynamic dance language.

DEPARTMENT OF INDIAN AFFAIRS

CANADA

CIRCULAR

OTTAWA, 15th December,1921.

IN YOUR REPLY REFER TO

No.

ALSO TO THE DATE OF THIS LETTER.

PLEASE WRITE ON ONLY ONE SUBJECT
IN EACH LETTER

ADDRESS REPLY TO THE
SECRETARY, DEPT. OF INDIAN AFFAIRS,
OTTAWA.

Sir,-

It is observed with alarm that the holding
of dances by the Indians on their reserves is on the increase,
and that these practices tend to disorganize the efforts
which the Department is putting forth to make them self-
supporting.

I have, therefore, to direct you to use
your utmost endeavours to dissuade the Indians from excessive
indulgence in the practice of dancing. You should suppress
any dances which cause waste of time, interfere with the
occupations of the Indians, unsettle them for serious work
injure their health or encourage them in sloth and idleness.
You should also dissuade, and, if possible, prevent them from
leaving their reserves for the purpose of attending fairs,
exhibitions, etc., when their absence would result in their
own farming and other interests being neglected. It is
realized that reasonable amusement and recreation should be
enjoyed by Indians, but they should not be allowed to dissipate
their energies and abandon themselves to demoralizing amusements.
By the use of tact and firmness you can obtain control and
keep it, and this obstacle to continued progress will then
disappear.

The rooms, halls or other places in which
Indians congregate should be under constant inspection. They
should be scrubbed, fumigated, cleansed or disinfected to
prevent the dissemination of disease. The Indians should be
instructed in regard to the matter of proper ventilation and
the avoidance of over-crowding rooms where public assemblies
are being held, and proper arrangement should be made for the
shelter of their horses and ponies. The agent will avail
himself of the services of the medical attendant of his agency
in this connection.

Except where further information is desired,
there will be no necessity to acknowledge the receipt of this
circular.

Yours very truly,

Deputy Superintendent General.

ABOVE: Letter from Duncan Campbell Scott, Deputy Superintendent General of the Department of Indian Affairs, sent out as a circular in December 1921. The letter advises the bureaucracy "to use your utmost endeavours to dissuade the Indians from excessive indulgence in the practice of dancing." Courtesy Heather Elton. *RIGHT*: The above letter was read aloud by Jonathan Fisher (*INSET*) in "Buffalo Spirit." Photos Heather Elton.

Creating Winds of Change
Introduction

Marrie Mumford
Chippewa-Cree
Director, Aboriginal Arts Program

As the lights in the Margaret Greenham Theatre fade to black, the sounds of a northern wind fill the theatre. A single, bluish light creates a circle on the stage, revealing, through the shadows, a drum dancer holding an Inuit drum towards the light. A single, synthesized sound pierces the whistling wind, and the statuesque drum dancer, standing on a rotating platform, begins to move.

With the first drum beat reverberating through the theatre, a cry is heard ... the beginning ..."Winds – creation coming out of the darkness ..." An Inuit drum dance is performed by Jeff Tabvahtah. This is the first piece of *Chinook Winds*, the first Aboriginal Dance Project at The Banff Centre for the Arts. It is opening night, August 30, 1996. The winds crescendo, and the drumbeat follows the cries of the dancer, flowing back, deep into the darkness of time, to the point of first contact. The pain of journeys that followed are exorcised to become a celebration.

I reflect upon tonight's performance – the result of a collective dream – one that has taken place over many years and many generations.

Photo Don Lee.

Chinook Winds

I hear the sounds of powwow and the drum of the Pipestone Creek Singers as they sing from "A Message for Our People." The stage is suddenly brightly illuminated, reminiscent of a hot summer's day, as people gather to dance. Six dancers in full regalia – Traditional, Fancy, Grass, and Jingle Dress – enter in pairs, each from a different direction, to begin *Four Directions*. Midway through this joyous dance the music becomes distorted, and the dancers begin to move in slow motion. A mysterious, mystical presence is heard as the sounds of throat singing rise in volume and the music changes to "Good Land – Throat Song" from the Throat Chants of Povungnituk, Canada.

The light of the northern wind transforms the stage as two Inuit dancers from the eastern Arctic enter from the Northern Direction – the place of the Bear, the place of healing. They dance through a column created by the powwow dancers, their throat singing blending with the songs of powwow. The dancers exit together with the power that comes from unity.

I barely have time to catch my breath before I hear the throbbing "electro-beat" of Russell Wallace's original and electrifying score for *Bear Dance*. I watch the exciting dance of Jeff Tabvahtah and I see, in this gifted young performer, the power and the grace of the Bear. Jeff's dance contains danger, rage, excitement, and … Bear humour.

An image of a residential school and Aboriginal children playing brass military instruments is projected onto the back screen of the theatre. The music for *Brass Orchestra* begins. It's the turn of the century – reserve life has begun. Dance is forbidden by the Canadian government; it is illegal and our drum, the heartbeat of our nations, is declared an instrument of the devil.

Brass Orchestra begins with a wedding procession led by a priest, played by Alexandra Thomson. She leads with a huge cross, a Bible, and a red, bleeding heart sewn on her black robe. The priest is followed by a bride, Sandra Laronde, and a groom, Allan Blake Tailfeathers, who dons a top hat for the occasion. Completing the procession are Jonathan Fisher and Dawn Ireland-Noganosh, each on trombone, Sylvia Ipirautaq Cloutier and Monique Diabo-John, on trumpets, and the most petite member of the company, Siobhán Arnatsiaq-Murphy on tuba. Daniel J. Secord, with great aplomb and seriousness, keeps the beat of the military drum – and occasionally, in moments of freedom, adds extra flourishes.

The performers are dressed elegantly for the wedding. In turn-of-the-century clothing they are shoeless with the exception of the priest. The piece is witty and very tongue-in-cheek. The priest keeps losing his grip on the very formalized and measured procession – as the group breaks out in wild jazz improvization, dancing, playing wonderfully, loudly, and very badly – but with great *chutzpah*. The priest regains his grip but you know with all that restless energy there, that it is not for long. The group poses for a picture, the priest smiles, the rest are serious, almost gloomy. The procession exits.

The lights come up on *Butterfly Dance,* a solo performed exquisitely by Tamara Podemski. The program describes the Butterfly Dance as a dance that portrays a woman's recovery from a period of mourning. Tamara is dressed in black regalia, with a shawl covered with ribbons of every colour of the rainbow – creating a swirl of colour as she moves. The music travels through time and memories, filled with yearning and longing for the past, but it does not stay there. It whirls us forward towards the future; to recovery, healing, creation … out of the darkness. A pause, and a women's traditional song, *Rejoice Mother Earth,* sung by the Pipestone Creek Singers, fills the peace of the moment. Six women, in full regalia, begin a Plains traditional dance, affirming women's connectedness with Mother Earth. They are led by Dawn, a traditional dancer for many years. She is followed by women dancing Traditional, Jingle Dress, and the Women's Shawl Dance. They move through space, intersecting one another, creating patterns that join to create a circle of Eagle fans – raised to honour the Grandmothers.

The three performances that follow – *Buffalo Spirit, Residential School for Boys,* and *The Duet* – celebrate Native resistance to the imposition of European culture. In *Buffalo Spirit,* Jonathan eerily evokes the image of the Ghost Dancers of the Plains people in the late 1800s. This image is juxtaposed with the reading of a confidential letter from the Deputy of Indian Affairs to advise the bureaucracy to "use your utmost endeavours to dissuade the Indians from excessive indulgence in the practice of dancing."

Residential School for Boys explores the attempted assimilation of children, forcibly taken from their families and communities. Russell's composition is haunting as it celebrates the power of memory to resist.

The Duet – Going Back Home is the story of the 1970s – a couple supports each other in a search for their cultural roots, gaining strength in an urban world.

Grand Entry – Intertribal and *Nungtsiaq – The Good Land* celebrate Aboriginal love for dance, the land, and the land's love for Aboriginal people.

Oka Female Warrior takes us to the 1990s. Images of survival are reflected in the text of "Northern Wind Song" by Morningstar Mercredi, performed by Tamara. Throughout the text, Sandra, as the ancestral Grandmother, weaves the song *Only She Is Beautiful*. This song, composed by the Red Bull Singers, is sung in Cree.

The final piece is a contemporary dance divided into three parts – *Dark Light, Red Belt,* and *Finale*. In the words of Alejandro Ronceria, choreographer for *Chinook Winds,* "… the final piece is a celebration of who we are …" It is a full company piece. *Dark Light* is about resurfacing from the darkness, hard times coming into the Red Belt. During the chinook winds, the pine cones in the tops of the trees turn red because of the warm wind forming what is known as a "red belt." This belt has occurred since the mountains have been standing. It will always exist. As Alejandro says, "It is such a beautiful metaphor for Aboriginal peoples because, although we are still fighting for many things, we are still here …"

Finale is a celebration of Aboriginal music, song, and dance. On opening night, the power and energy of this final ensemble piece brought the audience to its feet.

As the house lights come up I reflect on the many people who helped prepare the way for *Chinook Winds*. Those who, over many years and generations, made this project possible.

… As I contemplate the past with the future, I think of those who have gone on before us: René Highway, Larry Lewis, Jim Buller – to them and all who have had such an impact on tonight's performance, I am reminded of the lyrics to a song from Tomson Highway's *The Rose,* "… thank you for the love you gave …"

Hi hi from Sleeping Buffalo Mountain.

They Give Us Their Strength

Sandra Laronde
Teme-Augama-Anishnabe

With the *Chinook Winds* dance project, there were many discoveries by all of us. As an emerging stage actor, I have always been drawn to the stylized, choreographed movement that theatre affords. I wanted to be able to move easily on stage to choreographed movement, and to extend my physical vocabulary as a performer.

My passion for the "physical text" of theatre is clearly linked to growing up in Temagami, Ontario. I was involved in every athletic endeavour possible from track to hockey to table tennis – even jousting from canoes on Lake Temagami! Many of us growing up in smaller communities are very athletic, considering there are not a whole lot of opportunities for artistic development. It is not generally recognized that sports can be a starting point for dance, theatre, performance art, clown, and mask, among other possibilities.

Throughout the dance project, I learned delicate, softer, spiralling movement whereas

RIGHT: Opening ceremonies with the Round Dance Singers: Joe, Bruce, and Ellery Starlight. Video stills Richard Agecoutay.

Chinook Winds

before I had tended to gravitate towards angular, forceful corporeal movement. I realized that different images and emotions inhabit these finer crevices of movement. Alejandro would remind me to breathe and this would give an incredible vitality to movement. What interests me about "physical text" is the rich image life and memory that the body possesses. Though many of us have suffered great losses, our bodies continue to carry cultural memory, imagery, knowledge, and emotion. If trusted and approached with respect, the body has an infallible memory.

When Raoul Trujillo came for our final week before the performance, we grew a lot as a company. He enabled dancers to begin to trust and reveal the hidden expression of each movement. When the company was rehearsing, I remember Raoul saying "You need to look into the studio mirrors to ensure that your eyes see out and communicate an inner life. You'll notice when you look into the front mirror, you can also see into the mirror behind you." This creates the effect that there is a line-up of many of you. He added, "... these are like your ancestors behind you – dancing with you at this moment in time."

This honouring of our ancestry in contemporary expression reminds me of when I was first introduced to Japanese Butoh dance by master Natsu Nakajima. I became fascinated by the dignity and beauty that can come from a body containing great suffering. In Butoh, there is a departure from the masking of emotion and it is based on the personal and cultural expression of suffering and joy. I hear our own Native elders in the words of Butoh master Hijikata: "To live in today's world is to be surrounded by misleading symbols and tiresome conventions. There is a dark uneasiness everywhere. But we shake hands with the souls of those who have gone before us, and they give us their strength. This is the unlimited power of Butoh."*

Chinook Winds is in honour of the memory of René Highway, one of the first to fuse traditional and contemporary dance. I never met René Highway, but four years ago I dreamed he was walking behind me, smoking a cigarette in a white sports jacket with the collar turned up. We were walking on a difficult path leading towards a mountain top, dark against the blue sky, where glimpses of luminous bodies could be seen. This was a wordless dream, yet René, through his eyes only, conveyed that I was to remain on this particular path even though I could see where the shortcuts were. Every time I grew tired, I would look back, and René would be there, cheering for me with an incredible light from his eyes. There was such love there – so softly and powerfully communicated – that it inspired me to continue my journey with courage. Perhaps this dream foreshadowed the beginnings of the Aboriginal Dance Project in the mountains of Banff. I'm not sure. But I know that it touched me deeply, and René was "one that has gone before us" and has given much strength to a number of people that I have met.

My most memorable evenings were the spontaneous and dynamic discussions on Aboriginal dance. As a group, we learned about dancers like René. I noticed that this would happen when people from various communities came to visit. Jeannette Armstrong, Delphine Derickson, Raoul Trujillo, Karen Pheasant, Alanis Odjig, Amos Key, Olivia Tailfeathers, and the youth group, Karla Jessen Williamson and her family, among others, came. And, of course, when Marrie Mumford was present. Marrie worked tirelessly at organizing and creating a dynamic cultural community that was integral to the dance project. It also happened when we attended the Ermineskin powwow and other special occasions. We learned about our own dance and cultural history from the spoken word, and this was truly inspirational.

Some participants had years of dancing Traditional, Jingle Dress, Grass, and Fancy, and this contributed immensely to the program. Karen Pheasant, a traditional dance instructor and a champion Jingle Dress dancer, brought a lot of knowledge of women's traditional dances. Of all the women's dances, I was most drawn to Jingle Dress. This "healing dance" was literally given to an Ojibway woman in dream life. I hope to continue dancing Jingle at the revived Temagami powwow. Many of us will bring these dances to our own communities and perhaps even inspire others, especially the youth, to embrace these dances.

When we moved from traditional dance to contemporary dance, I had to literally "shake off" one dance form in order to go into the other. The body is held quite differently and moves to rhythm in a particular way, depending on the cultural influences. When dancing traditional, for example, there is a downward rhythm of the body towards the earth, which acknowledges our connectedness with Mother Earth. Aboriginal dancing, like martial arts, uses the body's natural abilities and momentum. It does not go against the grain of natural movement. In contemporary dance, and classical ballet in particular, it is more about reaching upwards. In order to get the proper form, you have to close the bottom of the rib cage, lift the chest, and lengthen the spine. There are other apparent paradoxes and bridges yet to be constructed in relation to the body and the dance world.

We also had the privilege of exploring Inuit masking with Karla Jessen Williamson, originally from Greenland. Karla had us moving impulse by impulse to the Arctic and Greenlandic Inuit drum, demonstrating fertility dances and creating fearsome masks as performers. The masking performer is a significant teacher in the communities, and there is much humour because this "clown" is incredibly physical and often tramples into the terrain of taboo. This early art form understands drama and comedy.

I am grateful for the opportunity to participate in the *Chinook Winds* dance project and to be in the mountains of the Sleeping Buffalo. With *Chinook Winds*, we continue to sow the seeds of soaring possibilities. This experience has helped me prepare for certain roles as a physical stage performer. I am also working on a solo piece in collaboration with a Toronto choreographer, tentatively entitled "Bush Lady," which will be presented in January 1998 in Toronto. The spoken text is inspired by the story of Ka Kita Wa Pa No Kwe, one of the oldest living Anishnabe women in Temagami, the "deep water" place and my home. The *Chinook Winds* project could not have existed if it were not for those who have gone before us, and those whose dedication and hard work have made this all possible. *All my relations.*

* *Viala, Jean.* Butoh. *Japan: Shufunotomo Co. Ltd., 1988.*

Raoul Trujillo

Raoul Trujillo is a mixed-blood Apache, Mexican, and French Canadian from New Mexico. He trained with the Toronto Dance Theatre and worked as a principal dancer and soloist with the Alwin Nikolais Dance Theatre in New York. He was an initial co-director and choreographer for the American Indian Dance Theatre. Significant works include *Maid of the Mist* (1990) and *The Shaman's Journey* (1988), as well as numerous shorter pieces, including *Desert Spirits Are Appearing*, *World Warrior III*, and *The Thunder Beings*. Raoul has pioneered contemporary Native dance in Canada and the United States. Trujillo also has an extensive acting career in theatre, television, and film. Theatre credits include *Royal Hunt of the Sun*, *Collected Works of Billy the Kid*, and *Equus*. Television credits include *Highlander*, *Sentinel*, and *Lonesome Dove*, to name a few. He was also the host of the excellent eight-part PBS documentary entitled *Dancing*. Trujillo has appeared in numerous films, including *The Adjuster*, *Black Robe*, *Clear Cut*, *Scanners II*, and *Paris France*. Most recently, he was part of the star-studded Native cast in *Son of Hiawatha*, where he played Hiawatha's antagonist Pau-puk-kee-wis. Heather Elton interviewed Raoul Trujillo about his involvement in contemporary Native dance.

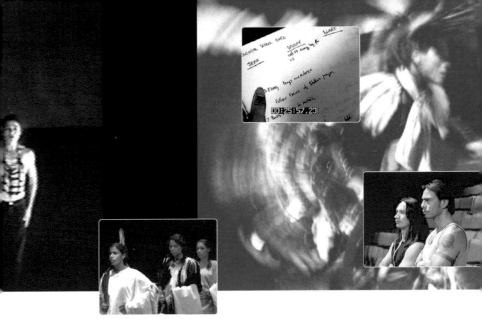

LEFT: During a chinook, the tree tops form what is known as a "red belt." This red belt has occurred since the mountains have been standing. It will always exist. We are like that red belt. (Left to right, front to back) Daniel J. Secord, Jeff Tabvahtah, Alexandra Thomson, Jonathan Fisher, Tamara Ceshia Podemski, Allan Blake Tailfeathers, Sandra Laronde in "Red Belt." Video still Michele L. *LEFT INSET*: Raoul Trujillo in rehearsal. Video still Richard Agecoutay. *CENTRE INSET*: Monique Diabo-John, Sandra Laronde, and Sylvia Ipirautaq Cloutier in "Women's Traditional." Video still Richard Agecoutay. *RIGHT*: Daniel J. Secord in "Grand Entry – Intertribal." A grand entry is the opening of a powwow when the dancers wear their finest regalia. Photo Heather Elton.
RIGHT TOP INSET: Dance rehearsal notes. Video still Richard Agecoutay. *RIGHT BOTTOM INSET*: Choreographer and Program Director Alejandro Ronceria (left) and Performance Technique Instructor Raoul Trujillo (right). Video still Richard Agecoutay.

interview

Is it true that the Aboriginal Dance Project and the desire to have a Native dance company go back to a vision you shared with René Highway and Alejandro Ronceria?

René and myself – Alejandro came much later – had this dream that one day we'd have a company. I worked with René for about 10 years before Alejandro joined us. René and I met in 1978 at the Toronto Dance Theatre. We definitely connected and started dancing together. Then I moved to New York to study with the Alwin Nikolais Dance Theatre and René followed. We shared an apartment on Bleeker Street. He was exposed to new dance forms and began to realize where he wanted to go with his work. René moved back to Toronto and started to bring his ideas into fruition at Native Earth Performing Arts. I danced with the Nikolais Dance Theatre for six years, toured the world, and taught the Nikolais technique.

In 1987, I joined René briefly in Toronto to dance with him in *New Song ... New Dance*, and then went back to New York to co-direct and choreograph for the American Indian Dance Theatre. That was the first attempt to create a Native dance company. I thought, perhaps, that company was the dream, but it wasn't. The producer wasn't interested in the investigative process of bridging the two worlds of traditional and modern dance.

So, René was doing his exploration into modern dance using Native ideas and legends, and trying to create a new movement language based on his emotional experience of coming from a remote reserve, from residential school, etc. A very unique experience that I didn't have, nor did Alejandro. So, that's what he was doing. I took on tradition and worked with powwow dancers

entirely in that language to develop a performance technique, based on traditional dance styles, that could be presented on the stage. I recognized that powwow was the arena for traditional dancers and sort of took advantage of that situation and said "Okay, let's take it to the stage now and share it with the rest of the world."

But, at that point it was all neon colours. Very untraditional, as far as the outfits were concerned. My intention was to take them back to their roots and get rid of the yarns. I conducted extensive interviews with elders to get the origins of the dances.

When my work with the American Indian Dance Theatre was over, I went back to Toronto, and this time Alejandro was there. It was 1988 and we began a journey that the three of us stayed committed to as long as we were together. After René died, Alejandro and I worked together until five years ago, when I embarked on an acting career. Although I still participated in dance and theatre, I've been out the loop. So this project is like a comeback into that world again.

Welcome back.

It is important for me to get back into the creative process and to share. This experience is amazing because the young dancers come from a similar background as when I started out. They have passion and an amazing talent, yet don't feel comfortable studying dance in a university. I had the same natural talent. So recognizing that, it is very important for me to share all the information I have to make it easier for them. That's our job as teachers – to illuminate the path for young people so they don't have to struggle as hard as we did. I came from a generation where you believed that you had to suffer.

No pain, no gain.

I don't believe that any more. I'm very impressed with the work that's happening here. Not only Alejandro's choreography and the work he's doing with these young dancers, but their openness and faith in us is admirable. I've worked with lots of people and run into incredible egos and resistance. There's none of that here.

Why is that?

Their passion to learn more of the art and to perform is so high that they don't take anything for granted. Some of them come from remote communities, where there are no outlets whatsoever to study dance, so they're grabbing onto this experience and sucking it all up. These people can't just take off and go to New York, or Toronto, to study dance. So it's been really empowering to be a teacher in that way.

They respect and trust you.

Yeah, and that's wonderful. Trust is the big word. I'm a visionary. I come from an ancient culture of song, dance, and storytelling. I believe I'm still doing that. In the past, dance came into the community because of a hunting expedition or something that happened, and the dance makers came forth and said "There's a dance that came to me in a vision," or however it came, and I believe we're doing the same thing today. We have that responsibility, and therefore shouldn't listen when people say "You can't do that." Crazy Horse would have done what he felt was right. It's no different today. Let's be teachers on a grander scale.

I want to talk about fusing contemporary and traditional dance forms. What strikes me as so remarkable about Chinook Winds is that the work refers to many different Native cultures, yet it never loses the integrity of each when bringing them together.

The challenge is immense. We're definitely committed to bringing in the traditional element, yet we're contemporary thinkers with ideas about who we are now. Right now, the challenge seems to be to try to bring them together, but I don't think that we need to do that. In *Chinook Winds*, you've got the contemporary movement and there are definite traditional pieces. You'll recognize steps from the Grass Dance or Fancy Shawl, but to truly merge them is not possible as they exist so entirely on their own.

You can incorporate traditional steps into a contemporary expression or form and it works, but traditional dance is something that is not defined just by the dance steps, but by the actual look of the clothing being worn. It's an attitude that goes with the particular dance. That can exist in its entirety. So, the only thing you can do is dissect that entity and do a modern piece. Take some of the feathers off and you've merged a bit. You can borrow some of the dance steps and use them in a new way. And you can say you've merged. Or, you can take some of the attitudes, but you can't truly merge them because they're so distinct.

I think Alejandro made a good decision to use the contemporary choreography in some of the narrative scenes, especially in Residential School for Boys.

Exactly. What it really comes down to, what's probably the best possible merge, is our history and our experience. And then bringing that into a contemporary form because it is abstract.

What was your involvement on Chinook Winds?

I was brought in primarily as the performance technique teacher to fine-tune the dancers. I can see what's lacking in a performance and I seem to be able to communicate to them what they need to do. As a teacher, I give a class that is not just about technique. I mean, I warm them up really quick. Get them on their feet and then take them beyond learning the steps into the realm of understanding what performance is about. I ask them to reflect on being in the moment and get them to take responsibility for the material and then project that out to an audience.

There has to be a certain level of confidence with knowing the choreography before they can do that.

To a degree. One of the things I was taught is that if you make a mistake when you're on stage, the audience will never know if you don't tell them. So, the idea is to stay in touch with the illusion you're creating. At a certain point they've got to trust that they know the movement, and just be in the moment. It's the experience of the now. You can forgive anything as long as you see honesty in performance.

When you arrived in Banff and saw your first rehearsal what did you think?

Actually, I was freaked out when I taught class. I thought "Oh my God. Poor Alex. This is rough." Particularly the men. Then I saw the work and I was totally blown away. Technique can be acquired later. Their talent is their passion and their artistry. As performers, they already know how to be there and command attention. It was absolutely riveting.

Chinook Winds seems to be a stretch for Alejandro. It's similar to Alejandro's *The Jaguar Project* in the sense that there are small scenes that move chronologically from traditional to contemporary times. The choreography seems more complex than his solo work.

Yes, but he comes from a classical background. Highly technical. It's natural for him to become task master and grand choreographer on that scale. It was a stretch for him to go the other way and do the solo work. I worked my butt off to get him to break out of the ballet mould. Actually, he told the dancers, "Oh Raoul is coming and he's going to break you down like he broke me down." But, I'm a lot more gentle now than I used to be. I have this real thing going on with ballet dancers anyway. They're just like little robots that don't even know what they're doing. They're just doing it.

Do you see references to your work, or René's, in the piece?

Anyone who knows our history can easily recognize elements of René, especially in the *Residential School for Boys* scene. There's the whole drumming section, because René was really fascinated with bringing drums into the work. And then there are whole sections of my work that came through like *The Shaman's Journey* and sculptural motifs. The drum section in the beginning, and even the whole exit, are borrowed from *The Shaman's Journey*. The slow motion section where their faces are used like masks reminds me of my work because I always felt that dancers' faces were neglected. So anyone who knew our work could see how we helped to influence each other. That's such a nice compliment.

Why is the Aboriginal Dance Project important?

The program provides an opportunity for young Native dancers to leave their communities, train as professional dancers, and experience the realm of theatre. The other more idealistic, but no less important, aspect is the preservation of the ancient traditions of song, dance, and storytelling. We are keeping them alive. But, we're also creating new stories. New dances. New songs.

RIGHT: Tamara Podemski in "Butterfly Dance." This Shawl Dance portrays a woman's recovery from a period of mourning. Photo Heather Elton. *BELOW TOP*: Christine O'Leary, Apprentice Assistant to the Choreographer. Photo Richard Agecoutay. *BELOW MIDDLE*: Alejandro Ronceria (left) and Raoul Trujillo (right) during dress rehearsal. Video still Richard Agecoutay. *BOTTOM*: Jerry Longboat, Daniel J. Secord, and Jeff Tabvahtah in "Red Belt." Photo Heather Elton.

Chinook Winds

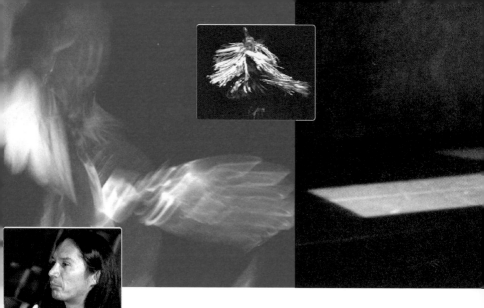

00:13:02.29

Alejandro Ronceria

Born in Bogota, Colombia, Alejandro Ronceria is a choreographer/director and film artist based in Toronto. Trained in classical ballet in Colombia, the Soviet Union, and New York, he has since danced with various companies and choreographers around the world. In Canada, Alejandro danced with the Karen Jamieson Dance Company in Vancouver before moving to Toronto to collaborate with René Highway and Raoul Trujillo. Since then, he has created artistically challenging work that explores Aboriginal culture and aesthetics. His own choreography includes *Ancient Rivers, Ayahuasca Dreams,* and *The Jaguar Project*. His recent work includes co-director/ choreographer for *New Voices Woman* and *Lupi, The Great White Wolf* for De-ba-je-mu-jig Theatre Group from Wikwemikong, Manitoulin Island, Ontario. Alejandro recently returned from a residency in Mexico City, where he worked with the Barro Rojo dance company to create a new choreography, *Prelude to Rain*. His second film, *A Hunter Called Memory*, premiered at the 1996 Toronto International Film Festival. Alejandro is the program director of the Aboriginal Dance Project at The Banff Centre and the choreographer of *Chinook Winds*. Heather Elton interviewed Alejandro Ronceria about the creation process of *Chinook Winds* and the new dance language emerging from the fusion of contemporary and traditional Native dance styles.

Chinook Winds

LEFT BOTTOM INSET: Alejandro Ronceria. Video still Richard Agecoutay. *LEFT AND TOP INSET*: Tamara Podemski in "Butterfly Dance." Photos Heather Elton. *ABOVE RIGHT*: Jeff Tabvahtah, Daniel J. Secord, and Allan Blake Tailfeathers in "Residential School for Boys." Photo Heather Elton. *CENTRE BOTTOM INSET*: Alexandra Thomson in "Dark Light." Video still Richard Agecoutay. *RIGHT BOTTOM INSET*: Sylvia Ipirautaq Cloutier and Siobhán Arnatsiaq-Murphy in rehearsal. Photo Richard Agecoutay. *BELOW*: Dawn Ireland-Noganosh, Alexandra Thomson, Siobhán Arnatsiaq-Murphy, and Monique Diabo-John in "Women's Traditional." Video still Michele L.

Chinook Winds is the inaugural project of the Aboriginal Dance Project. Has it been a success?

It is a big success and I feel really proud of my students. It was really challenging to put together all these people, from all these disciplines, styles, and cultures. It was really powerful to have Aboriginal teachers from all over Canada. In addition to music and drama, we taught contemporary dance technique and traditional dance – not only from the Plains, but also from Inuit culture. We taught history and literacy of dance. We worked really hard to produce a 70-minute show in four weeks. Even though the performance was a big success, the most beautiful thing was the process.

Did you arrive in Banff with the piece already constructed in your mind, or did you create the movement through improvisation with the dancers?

A bit of both. I am very methodical. A choreographer has a certain responsibility, so I had to do my homework. The project was a process that took a couple of years. The conception of the piece was already there before I arrived and I knew what I wanted to do with the movement. I asked the dancers to try things and if it didn't work I would do something else. I had to see what bodies I had to work with and see what their potential was, but because I knew who the participants were I started thinking about who could do what and how to get the best out of them. Often I had to choreograph four different sections at the same time. I have been learning to work with a lot of pressure; with no budgets and no time. That is when you are forced to manage your time really well. Every week I set up for myself an objective to finish a certain number of scenes. If I was on schedule I was laughing.

Did you write the narrative scenes, like *Residential School for Boys*, before you got here?

Yes, it has been part of my research for many years. Often, when I train emerging choreographers I give them scenes as tools to create movement. I invited Christine O'Leary here to be my assistant, because she wants to be a choreographer. So, I have been teaching her the process of choreographing and all the details of production. We need Native choreographers in this country. We need people who are thinkers, not followers. That is what I want to create.

The dancers come from many different Native cultures and while most have performed traditional Native dance styles, few have contemporary dance training. Did that present problems for you?

Yes and no. You have to take what people have. I've worked with trained professionals with a certain attitude that they can't do certain things outside of their particular training. It is very difficult to work with people like that because they refuse to take chances. So, when you have people who have never been trained, they sometimes do amazing things because they are open and they believe in what they are doing.

Considering the different cultural backgrounds and levels of technique, you did a good job of making them look like a company who have worked together for a long time.

The challenge is to make people coherent in the sense that they speak the same language. So, I designed a program with a bar that combined contemporary, classical, and traditional dance forms. After three weeks of training in new and hybrid movements, a certain alignment occurred. The dancers discovered a common ground and from there we progressed in different aspects.

Also, they worked so hard and there was tremendous commitment. As an Aboriginal person you know what the piece is about; what the issues are, what we are representing. What we are doing here is about us. We don't try to fake things. There is unity because people can identify with everything. It is an Aboriginal project, so you feel a big support, respect, and commitment. There's a lot of passion. They are coming here to work.

The dancers treat the stage as a sacred space.

I was trained that way and emphasize that through my training. That should be the way. I train the dancers throughout the whole process – not only to perform the steps, but what the steps are about. What's the importance of respect for each other. What's the commitment. These elements are all part of dance and ceremony.

The Aboriginal Dance Project offers a rare opportunity for those participants who live in isolated communities. I don't imagine most of them have done this before?

Never. There is so much talent in Aboriginal communities and people are just dying to do work. It's amazing.

Buffalo Spirit is very powerful. Jonathan Fisher moves like a ghost dragging the spirit of his culture across the stage. In a sense, he is dragging all that history and what happened to the people. He represents the past and the visions many of the elders had about what would happen. He is an ancient character with the voice of the present time. He knows what happened to the people therefore the scene comes right after the residential school sequence. Many of these dances were prohibited by the Canadian government and were not performed publicly for a long time.

The structure of *Chinook Winds* traces centuries of history, blending ancient creation myths, memories of residential schools, recent poems from Oka, to arrive at a powerful voice that celebrates the current cultural renaissance. There is this idea of remembering the past in order to know who you are today. What is the contemporary message?

The piece is about young people coming together and having these combinations of different traditional steps and putting it into a contemporary context. It's their voice now. It's about telling the story from different points of view without losing track of your history. We are making contemporary art. We are transforming the form to create a new dance style.

So, the message isn't that everyone is a modern-day warrior?

No, I'm not saying that, but that energy is there. You see these guys sweating and

having this power. But it's all about what I remember, and who I am, and reclaiming that. The final piece is a celebration of who we are as Aboriginal peoples. It represents emerging out of darkness; hard times coming into the Red Belt. During the chinook wind that happens here in Alberta the pine cones in the tops of the trees turn red because they receive different information from the warm wind. It has always been that way. It is such a beautiful metaphor for Aboriginal peoples because, although we are still fighting for many things, we are still here. We are going to remain here because this is our land.

Is it a problem that *The Good Land* contains movement from Alaska, yet the dancers are from the eastern Arctic?

The movement is not specific to only Alaskan Inuit. The piece is about fishing and hunting and the survival of the land. Without the good land you're dead. It is relevant to all Aboriginal cultures.

We are sharing and learning about diverse Aboriginal dance forms. That is our heritage. Even though it is a traditional dance done to contemporary music the meaning is still there. It is, not

Chinook Winds

only because we are Native, but what it implies to be Native. It is not just a word, but the whole thing behind it – culture, politics, land, survival. We can't avoid being political; we don't have a choice.

The Aboriginal Dance Project seems to come from a vision that has been around since the time of René Highway.
Yes, but not only from him, but from many of us who have been working for such a long time here. I was part of the planning and wanted to include all that I didn't have in my dance training in Colombia, the Soviet Union, the United States, and Canada. All about who I am. My culture. Although I appreciate classical music, I always wondered, When can I hear my own music? When can I wear my own outfits with our own aesthetic and designers? Perform our own dance steps?

Is Chinook Winds a bit of a departure from your previous work – The Jaguar Project, Ancient Rivers, and Ayahuasca Dreams – some of which has been solo work, or for fewer dancers, with content specific to South American culture?
I have worked all over the world with big companies, but have never had that chance in Canada. My work has not only been solo, nor is it specific to South American culture. *The Jaguar Project* incorporated symbols and creation myths from various Aboriginal communities. It also included languages from North, Central, and South America. *Ancient Rivers* involved three dancers and it represented contemporary Aboriginal identity from three perspectives, drawing parallels, again, between North, Central, and South America. Only *Ayahuasca Dreams*, a dance for four dancers, dealt specifically with South American ritual. I see *Chinook Winds* not so much as a

"Oka Female Warrior" rehearsal. Video still Richard Agecoutay.

departure, but a continuation in exploring Aboriginal themes and developing a movement vocabulary that is original and contemporary, but inspired and rooted in Aboriginal cultures and philosophies.

I am very comfortable working on a larger scale and have done so in the past. My background has been working with large companies in South America, Europe, and the Soviet Union. Most recently I choreographed a new work, *Prelude to Rain*, in Mexico City with a full company of 14 dancers and it was wonderful.

I feel that there is kind of a resistance in Canada to give independent choreographers the opportunity to work on a larger scale. With the exception of a few established companies and choreographers, that type of funding is difficult to get. Particularly if you are a choreographer experimenting with an Aboriginal dance language. One of the goals of the Banff program is to create more Aboriginal choreographers, not just dancers.

LEFT: Daniel J. Secord, Jeff Tabvahtah, and Allan Blake Tailfeathers in "Residential School for Boys." After centuries in existence, residential schools were finally closed in Canada in the late 1960s. However, child welfare agencies continued to keep families apart through their "scoop up" policy, taking Aboriginal children away from their families. Photo Heather Elton. *BELOW TOP*: The drum is the heartbeat of Mother Earth. *BELOW BOTTOM*: Alejandro Ronceria. Video stills Richard Agecoutay.

Journal Entry

Journal Entry

Siobhán Arnatsiaq-Murphy
Inuit

November 6, 1996 — We arrived in Banff on a Sunday. The weather was considerably warmer than I expected and I was enjoying the air-conditioned bus with its driver spilling out every known fact about Banff. I knew he gave this speech several times a day, every day, yet he didn't sound mundane, and from that I drew my first conclusion that there was something truly special about this land and this place. But that could've just been me and my romanticizing ways.

As we drove through the gates of Banff National Park I remember thinking, I have arrived, and it is wonderful. Since my acceptance into the Aboriginal Dance Project I wondered what experiences were in store for me at Banff, and in turn what I would make of them. Before the project even started I began to feel an awareness in myself, an awakening. I began the journey again, of walking within myself. I remember realizing that I hadn't taken a walk in a long time. Although I was thousands of miles away from the north, and had been travelling for two days, I had come home again.

Photo Richard Agecoutay.

Chinook Winds

With 12 participants in total, we began the rigorous schedule of dancing nine to five daily for five weeks. It was very tiring, both physically and emotionally, and throughout the five weeks we all had our moments. Many friendships were made and exchanged. Living together brought out all the strengths and the weaknesses we had to offer. Naturally, we had a few fights but even now I can look back on those times with fondness and longing. I don't know when it happened but somehow along

the way we began to think of one another as family and we truly were. Every participant had an important role to play, and we all acknowledged and respected that. I've learned to carry this over to my own family!

In the evenings, after a supper break and some free time, we returned to the agenda. We viewed dance videos as a group for several hours in our lounge. We

learned the history of dance and its various forms, a first for most of us. I enjoyed the viewing sessions. Although they were a part of the schedule it was our time to relax. I enjoyed learning about other cultures and the universal importance dance has in every culture. I'll gladly admit that prior to Banff and at the beginning of the project, I felt a certain lack of passion for dance with what I understood of it at that time of my life and what I had

LEFT: Siobhán Arnatsiaq-Murphy in "Nungtsiaq – The Good Land." This dance was inspired by Inuit Delta Drum Dancing. Photo Don Lee. *ABOVE LEFT*: Siobhán Arnatsiaq-Murphy and Sylvia Ipirautaq Cloutier in rehearsal. Video still Richard Agecoutay. *ABOVE RIGHT*: Siobhán Arnatsiaq- Murphy in rehearsal. Photo Richard Agecoutay.

been exposed to. I slowly felt its importance slip into my life. After all, for five weeks dance was my reality and my only tool. When I watched the videos in the evenings, I thought to myself, I can achieve that, I could someday be that. One of the videos we viewed was Alvin Ailey's *Revelation*. In a lounge surrounded by my peers I cried three times, shielding my face from the others, it was for only me to know. In my town there are no opportunities like the opera and the theatre, and here at this moment, I found what it is to be touched by a performance. I strive to reach that moment in my performing.

The Aboriginal Dance Project taught us all many things. It gave us a getaway, an opportunity and a positive outlet as individuals. For myself, I couldn't pinpoint exactly what it had given to me, but I felt it. I met some of the most inspiring people in my life. The daily experiences were all filled with a magic. We were all where we chose to be at that moment of our lives, and the colours were vivid.

Since returning from Banff, I have been involved with Sylvia Ipirautaq Cloutier in creating something very similar in my home town of Iqualuit. We are working with 15 youth in the training program *Performing Arts through Traditional Entertainment*, with 20 performers in total. In an attempt to empower the Inuit youth of Iqualuit we have been meeting three times a week. The youth are learning our traditional skills of throat-singing, drum dancing, square dancing, and our Inuit dance, and at the same time are being exposed to modern dance through Alejandro Ronceria, and with what we may have to offer. The mandate of the program is to deal with three important questions that elude many if not all Inuit and all Aboriginal cultures today: Where are we from as a culture? Who are we today as a culture? And where are we going as a culture? At a time when the largest Aboriginal land claim agreement in history (Nunavut: Our-Land) is being granted, and with the year 1999 creeping up rather quickly, I myself feel that I would like to instill in the youth many of the skills I gained from the Aboriginal Dance Project. The first dance performance takes place on November 22, 1997, and I look forward to

Sylvia Ipirautaq Cloutier and Siobhán Arnatsiaq-Murphy represent the North in "Four Directions," a dance that depicts the symbolic coming together of nations through traditional dance. Photo Don Lee.

watching our students in the spotlight. The program has been very successful, and the youth have taken to it quite well. They are being given a rare opportunity to challenge themselves, to discover who they are, and what their strengths are, as a culture and as individuals. They are given a moment where the whole town is at their feet, and where they have the chance to be heard. That is exactly what Banff was to me.

I see myself dancing in life for a very long time.

They Were Singing and Dancing in the Mountains

Iitaapasskaa Miistaki

Cheryl Blood
[Rides at the Door]

High along the chain of majestic Rocky Mountains that embrace the clear turquoise sky is an imaginary chiselled line – a border – that separates the United States and Canada. This is the traditional territory and land of the proud Blackfoot Confederacy. It is a place of rolling golden prairie, a thick emerald green carpet or snow white fields, depending on the season.

The weather brings both fierce blowing winds or warm chinook breezes, and silence so still you can hear the echo of a bird chirping. This is the home of Olivia Tailfeathers, Night Flying Woman (*Siipiipotakii*), member of the Blood tribe, and instructor of traditional songs, music, and dance for *Chinook Winds*.

Mother of four handsome sons, Olivia is a strong role model for her children and the students at *Tatsikiisaapo'p* Middle School,

Cheryl is a Kinaiki who lives on the Blood reserve in southern Alberta; she is also part Dene. An artist, writer, and actress, Cheryl promotes creativity as a healing process. Her educational background includes social work, business management, and writing.

Olivia Tailfeathers holding her son Lonny with Tamara Many Chiefs at a Flathead Powwow in Montana. Photo courtesy Charcouta News.

Chinook Winds

where she teaches music. From this environment she selects students for her group of Kainai Grassland Singers. Aside from her bright, smiling, beautiful face, Olivia can steal your heart away with her melodious voice and interpretative musical style.

Olivia's early music and dance influences began when her grandmother and mother, *otsitoi'paamoka*, sang lullabies. Her uncle Emil Wings and grandfather Emil Wings Sr. used to whistle *Nistsitapii* (Blackfoot) melodies and songs at night, tapping on the wall to keep the melody and rhythm. Olivia and her younger brothers and sisters fell asleep listening to different songs.

In mid-summer, during the Sun Dance, Olivia heard songs sung by the Buffalo Woman Society and the Horn Society and began to internalize these musical influences from Blackfoot culture. Traditional and cultural values permeated the environment. Not an active participant, knowledge was a silhouette of activity. Larger-than-life shadows of elders' movements danced on the walls while their song voices were carried by air, loud and clear as they sang throughout the night.

Living in two worlds, *Nistsitapii* and European, Olivia was also influenced by the Anglican church, where she was encouraged to become a choir member by the Reverend Stan Cuthand, who later became her mentor. He supported her by going to listen when she competed in public school music festivals. Olivia's eyes dance with delight as she remembers these happy memories that instilled strong values, a gift she shares by supporting musical endeavours of our youth.

Olivia also listened to Wilf Carter, Hank Williams Sr., Loretta Lynn, and Tammy Wynette because her father was an avid country and western music fan. She performed with local bands during the spring, summer, and fall at rodeos and other events.

Olivia has a traditional dance background and as a little girl she dreamed of owning a white tanned buckskin dress. In 1980 her dream was finally realized. This buckskin dress, which she was directed to sew from a Blackfeet lady in Browning, Montana, was proudly worn in the *Chinook Winds* performance. According to

Olivia, "This dress always seems to be worn by young women who want to dance. It is significant because the five hides have served a valuable purpose for young

"Ninastako" (Chief Mountain, Montana), sacred to the Blackfoot.
Photo Olivia Tailfeathers.

women to learn about their identity and to have pride in their cultural ways. Most people would be reluctant to share their dress with so many strangers because of the monetary value; however, it seems to have its own purpose because it has been shared with so many artists. There are times I have not recognized my own dress because it takes on its own beauty depending on the individual wearing it."

The first time Olivia was invited to the Aboriginal Arts Program at The Banff Centre she felt a lot of emotion and synchronicity in the old forgotten trails our ancestors travelled. She says, "En route I was moved by the stirring tranquillity in the hills and knew I had to be there. The gift of music was given to me and I felt I had to share my songs and music with the students. In exchange I would learn about the variation and styles of our music whether it be Mohawk, Oneida, Blackfoot, or Inuit."

As part of the community outreach aspect of the program, some of the *Chinook Winds* dancers attended our Sun Dance on the Blood Reserve and had the opportunity to hear sacred songs and drumming when members of the Horn society came out to dance. The sacred circle signified an understanding and a renewal in our unity as First Nations people.

At The Banff Centre, Olivia taught songs in Blackfoot that were her personal compositions, as well as sharing songs from the 1950s to educate the dancers about Blackfoot culture. They heard serenade songs from the Sun Dance and "Sacred Stone," a song given to the family of the late Ben Calf Robe, of the Siksika Nation. Olivia says, "I feel it is very important to teach our children about who they are and where they come from, so they know where they are going. Music and dance are the best ways we can learn about ourselves as *Nistsitapii* and I felt very honoured to be there as an instructor because it proved we were all one as the Creator's children. When I saw the performance of *Chinook Winds*, I cried because I could feel the spirits of our ancestors who have gone on."

The fusion of new and old inspired Olivia and I to return to our past. To research *Nistsitapii* song and dance we decided to interview various elders, a few who still remember when the drum first came to southern Alberta. It is with respect for our elders that we must confirm with them what we are writing about.

Late one evening, we drove to Lower Standoff, one of the oldest communities on Canada's largest reserve, to speak with Orton Eagle Speaker. We walked up to his old white house and gently knocked on the door. No one was home. Just as we were leaving, a big truck came speeding into the driveway. Inside was Orton, his wife, grandson, and great-grandson. He got out and quietly said he had to take his grandson to town, and then he'd rush back because he knew we would be here. He came back and as his wife prepared tea and banana bread, his great-grandson with the blue eyes kept teasing him, and I could tell he had Grandpa wrapped around his baby finger. Orton confidently, and with pride, began to tell us stories about his involvement with song and dance.

Orton Eagle Speaker is a rare, kind, generous, intelligent man, father, grandfather, and great-grandfather. He honoured us both by sharing with us a lifetime of learning. He told us many stories.

"Historically our songs and drumming originally came from different societies and, therefore, they were ceremonial," he said. "We had many different societies: Black Tail society, Brave Dog society, Mosquito society, Yellow Pigeon society, Magpie society, Skinny Horse society; others too numerous to mention, and most have died off. We have lost many of our dances from the past and if we could bring back some of our elders who had the knowledge we could revive these dances. We had many different dances from our societies before the Mandans (Earth Dwellers) and Kaispai gave us songs and dances."

Orton told us that social drumming and singing originally came from the Omahas when the Kaispai visited their traditional territory and observed them singing and dancing around a fire. He said, "When Blackfeet raiders went to Kaispai territory and came back home, they held a dance. In later years, the Mandans came up to Lethbridge, it was just a small town then in the 1800s. Somewhere around Weasel Fat Flats, near the medicine wheels, it was the first snow storm in September, a deep wet snow but not cold, one man got up to get firewood to start a fire and when he sat down to take a rest he saw some people across the river, on the hills wandering around. He invited them over – I cannot remember if it was two men and one woman, or two women and one man – anyway they spoke English.

"When they began to talk, the Mandans said, 'We came to give you some war dances, an Owl Dance, Rabbit Dance, Round Dance; these are free. We also have some articles for the dance: whip, drums, eagle bustle, bone whistle, hand drums, woman and man trailing headdress; these items you will have to pay for. Invite all the people and we will demonstrate the dances.' Some riders went around to Old Agency, Standoff, and headed south from there to invite people to the dance, which was to be held in four days. An explanation was also given to the people about payment for the articles."

In four days, numerous people had gathered. "The dance was packed and some of the people couldn't get in," Orton said. "The Mandans told stories about how and why each dance came to be. War dances were done before people go on a raid and, when successful, another dance is done. Kaispai and Mandans were dancing years before us.

"In the past, before the time of powwow, women sat on one side of the room and men on the other. In the Round Dance, or women's dance – *Aki Paskan* – people go to honour people and they would dance in doubles. There were a few people who didn't know how to dance so they danced by themselves and that is how the Round Dance started. Owl Dance is always a woman's choice and when the man sits down, he would go and pay her because she demonstrated honour and out of respect he would return these values. It's a custom you don't see any more these days."

Orton remembers that the Mandans also brought with them the first large powwow-style drum. "Mandans brought over the big drum, *Omahkisttokimaa*, designed with eagle claws on one side, and was painted yellow and red on the other side, representing day and night," he said. "Over a 100 horses were given in payment for the articles they brought with them. The Mandans brought them to Lethbridge and sold them to pay for their train tickets back to North Dakota. We, the Bloods, paid for our dances and that is how we got them. I do not know how the Stoneys, Sarcees, and Crees got their dances."

ABOVE LEFT: Dawn Ireland-Noganosh in "Grand Entry – Intertribal." *ABOVE RIGHT:* The Round Dance Singers perform at the ceremonies on opening night *(left to right)* Joe, Bruce, and Ellery Starlight. Video stills Richard Agecoutay.

Chinook Winds

Orton Eagle Speaker is a traditional songwriter who has composed hundreds of songs. We asked him about his creation process and about ownership protocol. He said, "Some songs come in dreams or visions, or you can fast. My uncle George Shields – *Naatoisaopoi Natoisaopoi* (Sacred Plume Bonnet) – would go and fast sometimes four to eight days without food and water. He would have every animal represented on his sacred war bonnet. I hear stories about 5, 10, 20 people going to fast in the mountains together and I have to laugh because in the past you would go and fast at Chief Mountain by yourself.

"Traditionally, songs come from dreams, visions, and ceremony. The holy songs and powwow songs were passed through lineage. Honour songs were passed down through various societies.

"While most songs are passed on through lineage, a person may be honoured by the owner and thereby given a song directly. Great-grandfathers to grandfathers, fathers to sons and, yes, some songs are women songs too. Some of the songs I made I keep – especially Honour songs. My daughter asked me for an Honour song for her son, my grandson, and I gave him a song and gave it to her on a tape to keep it for him so that when he is older he can learn it and use it. My uncle made a song and I keep it and no one else can use it.

"My friend from the United States visited me one summer and told me 'I will give and teach you some appraisal songs.' Appraisal songs evaluate the worth or significant accomplishments of an individual. They set status or value of an individual. He said, 'I will teach you 5 now, and when you come and visit me I will teach you 8 more, and that will be 13 songs in total.' Well, he taught me the 5 songs that summer, but he died before I made it to see him. I don't know if anyone else knew those songs, but he died with 8 more he was going to teach me. Cree, Blood, Blackfoot, and Blackfeet, you have to go through ceremony to sing appraisal songs."

We asked Orton if he remembered when words first started to be used in songs. He said, "Our ceremonial songs were the only ones I remember having words in the beginning. In the past, just straight songs were used and then the Kaispai began to tape songs with words and that's how we started to use Blackfoot words in songs. Different tribes, the Bloods, for example use Blackfoot and English words 'When the dance is over I will take you home, honey, on my old grey mare, hiya aiya ...' and the Cree do that too."

Orton thinks that some songwriters today no longer approach the material with the same cultural values. "I used to sing a lot. I would make songs. Nowadays, we have copycats who don't make their own songs. I wonder, do they know what they're singing about? When I make songs I usually put together four or five songs and once I get a song to be a good song, then I put it to a drum. I use the rhythm. A lot of singers don't have the rhythm, you can tell when you get up to dance. The main singer, or start singer, is the rhythm and if a group doesn't have the rhythm they are no good.

"This young man once came to me and told me he was a good-time singer. I thought to myself, then he should know all the different society songs, because that's what a good-time singer is. Anyway, I went to Heart Butte, Montana, for a powwow and this man, George Old Person, he is deceased now, he came to me while I was sitting in the bleachers and he said, 'Come and sing with our drum.' I was happy to sing with them. I sang with the Star School Drummers at this ceremony. George Old Person went to this group of Levern singers and asked them to sing a Fast Race Horse Society song and none of the drummers knew it. I knew it and I offered to sing for them. When the singing was over he threw $60 on the drum and said split it with your singers. I never got one cent for singing for them even to this day. When you call yourself a good-time singer and are requested to sing you should know all the society songs."

And, listening to the stories of this humble man we knew that his memory is precious and extends far into the past. "The first Rabbit Dance song was brought from the South Dakotas around Pine Ridge area," Orton said. To prove his point he sang us the first Rabbit Dance song and it was so beautiful I ached deep inside and felt emotion stirring, then rising, until I choked back tears of sorrow, joy, loneliness, and, finally, peace. At this moment, no other singer could compare. Orton's song was the language that reached and spoke to our souls.

Daniel J. Secord in traditional regalia in "Grand Entry – Intertribal." Video still Michele L.

Chinook Winds

Russell Wallace

Russell is a Stl'atl'imx musician and composer who works in western and Aboriginal electronic musical forms. He studied Performing Arts at Spirit Song Theatre School and Information Technology at Capilano College, both in Vancouver, B.C. He has written original scores for films by Loretta Todd and videos by Dana Claxton, as well as several plays. He has appeared as a musician on numerous CDs and cassettes and composed the music for a video game. Heather Elton interviewed Russell Wallace about music in Lillooet culture and in *Chinook Winds*.

ABOVE: Russell Wallace composing the music for *Chinook Winds* in the Electronic Audio Recording Studio at The Banff Centre for the Arts. Video stills Richard Agecoutay.

interview

Chinook Winds

What role does music have in your culture?
In the Lillooet culture the music and songs belong to clans and to certain families or individuals. They are passed down within that clan. And a lot of the music is based in ceremonies, so it is sacred and only certain clan groups and families can sing those songs.

Do the songs have specific functions?
There was some sacred music, some of which I don't know. The music my mom sang all the time was family stories. A lot of songs told stories. There were social songs about going out and picking berries or fishing that were sung mostly at social gatherings, funerals, and weddings. If you were asked to sing, you got up and sang a song. It wasn't tied in with any ritual or ceremony.

On the west coast, because songs are sacred, they had to be sung a certain way with no room for error. But within the Lillooet, because there wasn't that restraint with the ceremony on certain songs, it became more open and because of that there are a lot more songs that have harmony in them, which is not really present in a lot of other cultural groups in that area. Within a lot of the cultural groups around here, there's the one voice, but within ours there could be two or three voices happening at the same time.

In our group the women play a strong role in the music and are the ones who kept all the songs going. My mom is the song keeper. She and my sisters do all the singing. I notice in a lot of other cultures that the men were the ones who kept the music and sang the songs.

What kind of instruments are used?
The hand drum is the most important instrument. A few drums were made in sort of a square shape but not a lot of people make them any more. There was a time when logs were used for percussion as well. The music was all vocal and percussion.

How did you get involved in contemporary music?
Well, I've always liked music and I learned the guitar when I was really young, so I played that off and on through my teenage years. But I don't really think of it as a career. I got involved in radio at high school, where we ran a student show. At that time there

was no Native radio programming, so I approached the Native Communications Society of B.C. and Vancouver Co-op Radio to put together a Native program. And so we got that started, but the problem was finding the content. There was a lot of political content, but the music wasn't available. Recordings did happen in the 70s and were released on vinyl, but they weren't widely distributed.

I've always been interested in synthesizers and computers and when I had enough money I bought an Atari because that was the major music computer at that time. I started sequencing and sampling on the computer and then got involved with a couple of groups that did a lot of that stuff.

Native groups?

No. Electronic industrial bands in Vancouver. I guess I was more into techno pop. *Front 2 4 2* and *Ministry* and those kind of sounds. *Skinny Puppy*. I hung out with the whole Nettwerk label scene that started in the mid 80s. A lot of their artists were electronic-based at that time, but then they moved more into the contemporary folk thing with *The Grapes*

of Wrath and Sarah McLachlan. We just fooled around and started our own label, Spiral Records. We released two compilations and some independent tapes and CDs of Vancouver artists.

Did you receive funding?

No. We did it on our own. Independent. We got some support from the radio stations, but we didn't get much distribution. We had a few deals with other independent labels across Canada where we distributed and promoted their artists in Vancouver and they would promote our artists in Toronto. At that time there wasn't a lot of distribution for techno music and the distributors we did approach weren't very nice. The deals weren't very favourable to independent stuff.

Can you explain the structure of the score for *Chinook Winds*?

Well, in talking with Alejandro and looking at dancers from across Canada, our approach was to incorporate the traditions and sounds of Aboriginal people into a contemporary sound. So there is a lot of sampling, taking the songs that they sang, or the instruments that they used, and sampling them.

Did you compose with old instruments like deer hoof rattles?
No, not this time. I've worked with them before though. The composition is more in a contemporary vein. The instruments used are all electronic.

Do you record traditional instruments and then file them electronically?
Yeah. I worked on Margo Kane's *The River-Home*, which was produced here at The Banff Centre, and we had a lot of traditional instruments and I did sample them. The Aboriginal Dance Project only had hand drums, and The Banff Centre doesn't have any traditional instruments here, so it's kind of hard to get a hold of any. So, on *Chinook Winds* I sampled a lot of the singing. A few of the dancers knew songs and taught the other ones, so I got them to sing as a group in the studio.

What other sounds are on your score?
A lot of it is electronic-based synthesized sounds. Some of it is sampled, like traditional and western instruments like the violin and orchestral instruments. Chiyoko Szlavnics played saxophone on a couple of songs.

Did you compose music specifically for each scene in the dance, or did you work on a full-length piece?
I talked to Alejandro and looked at the choreography and tried to match the music with a particular scene. So each scene is separate from the other.

How did you integrate the Inuit music?
That was one we had a few problems with. I wasn't sure what they were doing or what Alejandro really wanted, so I brought the dancers into the studio and they sang for a while and I developed a lot of source material from that.

And Jeff Tabvahtah plays his drum?
Yes, he plays the drum along with the music at the beginning of the piece. Alejandro wanted his drum to be the focus and the music to support him, so there are no rhythms in that song. It's mostly sound effects like wind.

Did you record the wind?
That came out of the sound-effects library at The Banff Centre.

Have you taped any sounds in nature?
No. I would like to though, there's a lot of really interesting sounds here. There's all this stuff we could use, but I didn't have any time to do that.

Did you use powwow songs to accompany the sections in the piece with traditional dance?
Alejandro chose the songs for those parts.

How did you approach the *Residential School for Boys* scene and the more dramatic or narrative segments?
For *Residential School for Boys*, I used a song my mother sang. It's a Lillooet song that's about a grandmother whose daughter had passed away, and she's responsible for her grandchildren. The song tells a story that she has to walk around without any shoes and has to carry these two children and there's nothing left to eat except the backbone of a fish. It was really powerful for me and I thought if I sampled one section it would

be like a memory, like the residential school, where even though you were forced to speak another language that you had never heard before and you couldn't sing your songs any more, and you couldn't do dances any more, the memory is still there. I can remember my mom talking about being in residential school and when the nuns weren't around, they would teach each other songs.

So, the memory is still there, the very memory of the song, the memory of the language, even though you might not be using it, it's there on your tongue, it's there in your throat. I wanted to approach it that way. So I've taken her voice and put it with western music reminiscent of

hymns. Then, I added my own voice on top and improvised on my mother's melody. By taking a tradition and moving it, having the background of western music and incorporating my voice, it suggests that the culture is still there but changing. The language is changing, it's not static, it keeps moving. That's how I approached that.

Composing the score for *Chinook Winds* must have been very challenging as it pulled together so many diverse elements?
Each project I do is very challenging because I don't have training in music. Incorporating Native music into an electronic sound is actually not that difficult because I think a lot of the electronic music happening today is sort of based on traditional music, whether they realize it or not, because it's all based on repetition. The beat is like the drums.

Did you work in 4/4 time?
Yeah, it's all 4/4 time. There's one piece where it's in 3/4 time, but everything else is done in 4/4. That facilitates the use of traditional music because a lot of it is based on 4/4.

Tell me about working with your mother and the types of collaborations you've done.
She sang all her life. It's just recently that she's been getting work doing voice-overs

for film. We've worked in traditional music, and I've worked in contemporary music, but together we try to create new songs based on traditional songs that have the same song structure by writing new lyrics and new music. The music is all vocal work, but it's based on the traditional form. So we're writing traditional music.

Can you explain what that form is?
It's based on the vocal styles of Lillooet. There's a lot of melody and there's some

Video stills Richard Agecoutay.

harmony to it as well, but it is based on 4/4 time. Each song is different unto itself. I remember a song my grandmother sings, there's a part in the middle where she sang one word and it goes on beyond the 4/4 time, then in the middle of the song it goes over to a different rhythm, it goes back in two to get that phrase in. That one is difficult to sing. Only my mom can sing it. When my family sings with her they stop and let her sing that one, actually, because the word is sort of difficult to say as well. Our language has about 56 different consonants and a lot of it is guttural or throatal, a lot of the tongue. It's a real difficult language actually.

If you write new lyrics and new music, wouldn't that be a completely new song, or is there some underlying structure that you could still recognize?

The songs are very beautiful, melodious, and so the music I create from uses some of the melody, one or two notes end up changing melodies. Melody and harmony are the parts that stick out when I listen to the music.

Here you are in a state-of-the-art recording studio. Where did you learn to use this stuff?

It was at Capilano College. I'm still there actually. I went through the Information Technology program, which looks at CD-ROM production and interactive design.

Did you compose the score for *Chinook Winds* on a Macintosh?

Yes, in a program called Studio Vision. My mother's voice was sampled onto one of the sequencing tracks and then I have three tracks of keyboards. My voice came in through Pro Tools, which is a digital recording, a hard disk recording device. We ran it through two Macintosh computers, one of the computers dedicated to the sequencing. The two computers were synched up with SMPET and we recorded onto DAT, which is digital audio tape. So a lot of time was setting it up.

Technology has always been of interest to me. But you don't have to be familiar with a computer to do the music. If you're a singer you just have to practice your voice and your voice is with you, you don't have to be dependent on the technology, whereas I'm totally dependent on technology for my music, which says a lot.

Is there a technique to learn how to sing?
Those are the ceremonial or sacred music. It helps to be in touch with your body and to know what your limits are so you don't ruin your voice. My mother has always sung and my grandfather played a lot of instruments. I would call myself a hereditary musician in the same way that some people call themselves hereditary chiefs or hereditary medicine people. I'm a hereditary musician, it just came. And I think a lot of Native people have it in them to sing.

What responsibilities do you have as a hereditary musician?
It's nothing formal, it's just something that I like to think of. The responsibility is to keep singing the songs. My children are very into songs and my nieces and nephews are learning the songs.

How many songs do you know?
Maybe about a dozen. But my mother knows quite a bit more than that.

When she composes new songs, contemporary songs, does she prepare herself in any way?
Well, we do it together, we sit down and talk about it and we play around with different melodies and she speaks the language, she finds the appropriate words. There were two songs that we came up with and they were both used for different film projects. Actually, the first piece that we collaborated on was Loretta Todd's film *The Hands of History*, and that was the woman's Honour Song, which comes in at the beginning of the film. We came up with the melody and she came up with the words for the piece. The second one we've done was for a new film by Loretta Todd called *Forgotten Warriors*, about Native war veterans, so we came up with a Warrior Song and that one has no specific lyrics to it, it's just sort of vocalization.

You have plans to record the songs that belong to your family. Is that because you want to preserve them in a more permanent medium than oral tradition, or is it just a project that interests you and you have the ability to do it?

It's for both reasons. My mother knows so many songs, and because she's coming to later parts of her life, I think it's really important that we have them. And it would be useful especially in the schools around the Mount Currie and the Lillooet area to have access to the songs. But I want to produce it in a professional studio with mikes and digital tape, the digital medium, and have it mixed with different effects and viewed from a contemporary perspective.

Would you actually add tracks and mix them like you've done with the Residential School for Boys song, or leave them as raw documentation of your mother singing?
I think we will do two different ways. One is to have the documentation done and then work from that using instruments like the piano and saxophone to play the same parts, but improvise on top of it. I've heard it done a couple of times and I think it sounds really cool. And I think that's something we can do; like having the traditional, just the voices and the drums, and then contrasting that with interpretations of that on piano, or synthesizer, or a contemporary western instrument.

RIGHT TOP: Tamara Podemski. Video still Richard Agecoutay. *MIDDLE*: Russell Wallace in the recording studio at The Banff Centre for the Arts. Video still Richard Agecoutay. *BOTTOM*: "Red Belt." Video still Michele L.

Chinook Winds

Jeff Tabvahtah

Jeff is from Arviat, a community 200 kilometres north of Churchill, Manitoba. Arviat is in Nunavut, formerly the Northwest Territories. He comes from a very traditional community where drum dancing and other activities were introduced to him at a young age through elementary school. To this day, the elementary school continues cultural immersion with elders from the community.

Jeff didn't drum for many years, and it was only when he turned 15 that he touched a drum. Since then, he has learned different kinds of drumming and dancing, as well as learning how to make a drum through his great-uncle.

interview

While attending school in Ottawa, Ontario, in 1994/95, Jeff was invited to model Inuit clothing for *Qaggiq '95* at the Museum of Civilization in Hull, Québec. The clothing was designed by Inuit women, including Jeff's mother. He was then invited to perform at the Canadian National Exhibition in Toronto, modelling in a choreographed fashion show directed by Alejandro Ronceria, at the Inuit Spirit of the Arctic pavilion in 1995. In February 1996, Jeff again did a fashion show at the Museum of Civilization for *Qaggiq '96,* directed by Alejandro Ronceria.

Jeff currently teaches adult education courses in Inuit history, math, English, and life management skills through the high school in his community. He hopes to get further involved in theatrical arts and to continue his education. Heather Elton interviewed Jeff Tabvahtah about the tradition of drum dance in Inuit culture and his experience in *Chinook Winds.*

Tell me about the tradition of drum dance in Inuit culture, the different kinds of drums that exist, and the techniques and style of drumming.
The whole thing behind drumming is the idea of celebration. It was also used by shamans when they were calling for help, from their helping spirit, which might be a bear, or whatever – their *Tornga*; that's what they call it. Shamans would go into an igloo or tent and use the drum to help get them into a trance so they could travel to different worlds to ease or conquer demons or spirits that troubled their tribe.

My own interpretation of *qilauti*, the Inuk drum – this probably isn't the right definition of the word, but the word *qilak* means "heavens." The word *qilauti* might be the shorter version of the word *qilungmurruti*, which means "object used to get to the heavens," so *qi lau ti* to my way of thinking also means "object used to get to the heavens."

When you drum, the reason you start off slow is because you're like this mythical Inuk beast that flies and drops caribou from the air and they die when they hit the ground. To me, that's what it's like using the drum; starting off slow is like the beating of your wings. And beating and beating, you get faster and faster, as you get higher and higher. And the screams are of joy or of pain. And finally, you get to the heavens, you either just stop or slow down to show that you're going back down.

LEFT TOP: Jeff Tabvahtah in rehearsal for the opening number, "Winds." Video still Richard Agecoutay. *LEFT BOTTOM:* Photo Richard Agecoutay.

Are shamans still active in your
community?
No. The last one that I know died in the
early 80s. People were scared of them.
There were certain qualities that might
suggest that the child should be a
shaman like if they were born with teeth,
or hair.

Shamanism has always been kind of
mysterious. Shamans were very strange
and secretive. Only shamans understood
the way of life of the shamans. They even
had their own language.

The community I come from is still
very traditional, but it's also very
religious. It's kind of intertwined with
Christianity, so shamanism was thought
of as demonic. After the arrival of
Christianity, the practice was forgotten
or shunned.

Does using the drum to journey for the
purpose of healing interest you?
I've grown up around Christianity so, no
it doesn't interest me. I like to believe
that we're all equal, and the idea behind
being named after someone that's come
before you and they're there to help you.
And just being a part of life and not

taking anything for granted. And having
to rely on yourself to do things. And that's
what they teach when you grow up in Inuit.

Many people mistake Inuit and other
Native people of Canada to be alike. But,
we're very different. Inuit have a very
different view of life and culture from
other Native groups in Canada. In the
Inuit culture, there is no Creator because
everything is equal. You are no more
important than any other living animal
because that animal serves its purpose
and you serve a purpose. There is no one
powerful being; everything is the same.
Out of respect for the animal, if we are
the same, you treat everything as if it
were as important as you, and it, are – all
living things need each other because we
are all part of the circle of life.

Who do you give thanks to then if there
is no Creator?
There is Sedna, who is not really a god. It
happened a long time ago. There's this
family in a boat. A storm comes up and
the boat sways from side to side. There is
danger that the entire family will drown
because most Inuit don't know how to
swim. So the man throws his daughter,

Sedna, overboard and in desperation she grabs on to the side of the boat. Her father doesn't want his daughter on the boat because she weighs too much and he thinks she will tip it over. So he takes his snow knife, his spunner, and cuts her fingers off. And she sinks to the bottom of the sea. Her fingers become the animals of the sea.

So when there is no game, the hunters say Sedna is upset and all the animals are tangled in her hair. A shaman has to go down in the deep water and comb her hair because she has no fingers to comb it with. So the shaman uses the drum and he goes off to find Sedna. He has to be very careful. And he combs her hair, makes her at ease, and lets all the animals out. Then the community can go hunting again. Inuit used to be, and still are, very superstitious. Usually when hunting was bad it was blamed on the community because a number of taboos may have been broken.

When you kill an animal and use the skin to make a drum, do you give thanks to the spirit of the animal?
There's an old Inuit tradition that when you kill a seal you let the blood flow back into the sea through the hole in the ice to give thanks because you're rewarding the seal for giving itself up to you. And you put water inside the animal to help the spirit because it's thirsty. Put some fresh water in your mouth – some snow or ice – and melt it. From your mouth you pour it into the dead seal. That's quenching the thirst of the seal.

Do you always use caribou skin for the membrane?
I always use caribou, or fabric. In my region there are tons of caribou. We are Caribou Inuit. Caribou is an important part of our life. Caribou is mainly used on drum membranes. The reason I don't use caribou for things like *Chinook Winds*, where I use my drum every day for a long time, is because caribou is very delicate. It has a beautiful sound but it takes a lot of work to prepare. I have to wet it, tighten it, and have to allow it to dry. Then I can use it. With fabric there's no need for that. I just stretch it and it's ready to go. With a caribou drum, if I happen to miss the rim and hit the skin it stretches, so I have to wet it again,

tighten it. But with this fabric if I hit it I can just tighten it. I don't have to do all the work. And it preserves much better.

How many different kinds of Inuit drums are there?

I'm not sure about Siberia and Alaska. In the western Arctic, drums are about two feet in diameter, maybe two and a half. They're the Delta Drummers. They have a long stick that's equal or longer than the diameter of the drum and it's got a curve to it, so what they're actually doing is hitting the rim and the membrane at the same time. And it's got a very, very beautiful sound.

The drums from the central Arctic, or Kitimiut, are larger than ours. I don't know what the whole belief is behind it, but the rule for them when they're making a drum is to have it three arm-lengths long. They have a huge handle that goes all the way down their arms and their elbows to use as leverage. They play very slow. On the frame, the two sides and the edges. They play the same way we do.

The drum from Greenland is smaller, about two feet in diameter. It's got the same principle as our drum. The way they play is to swing it back and forth.

It's right up by their face when they sing.

In the eastern Arctic, which is my region, the diameter of the drum is about three feet, and the full length of the wood used to make the drum is one arm-length and a half.

Is drumming connected to a song, or storytelling?

Always. We never drum silently, except for what I do in *Chinook Winds*. Where I come from, drumming is a form of storytelling. You write your own song about your experiences, or how your family is, and stuff like that. I use my drum every time there's a celebration and even not for celebrations, just to get together with the elders to share old songs. This is my father's song. This is my song at this time when I went hunting one time. This is my song when there was hardship. That's what the elders do, just get together and share songs to refresh their memories of when they were younger. And have some fun.

Do people own the songs they make?

Yeah. The songs don't have titles like "The Wind Blowing," instead it's called "This Person's Song." That's the way all songs go. All your relatives know your song. These songs are like poetry, like Japanese haiku, in that they don't rhyme but they sound good when they're sung.

And so history is shared through the songs. Family songs are passed down from generation to generation. My great-uncle, who taught me how to make my drum, also told me I had to teach my song to my mother, so she can sing it. You teach it to your mother or your wife so she sings it while you drum. It's too difficult to sing and drum at the same time.

Are you a hereditary drummer?
Well, all Inuit drum. I don't know about Inuit in northern Québec. I think they lost their drumming quite a while ago, but where I'm from every family member has drummed at some point. My grandparents' parents.

I'm the youngest one because it's becoming very rare. It's not seen as cool. Younger kids are embarrassed because it takes so much practice to become good. Way back when, it was easy to start drumming because we're a small community, like a clan, and everybody knew everybody else. There would never

be more than 30 in this clan. You would just get up and drum and people would understand, that it's his first time and he'll get better. Today, 80 per cent of the population is under 21 years of age.

If someone were to try to drum they would go "Haahh, you can't drum." It's intimidating because so many people are watching. And Inuit are naturally shy.

The kind of drum dance you do is extremely physical. The entire body is engaged in beating this enormous drum slowly at first, then with a rapid pulse. It's very powerful.
I dance very different from other drummers in my community. From where I'm from,

Sylvia Ipirautaq Cloutier and Jeff Tabvahtah in "Nungtsiaq – The Good Land." Photo Don Lee.

the way they dance is like the way we speak. Slow and relaxed, but all Inuit that drum start slow and build up to a quick beat that sometimes just stops at the end of the song, or they slow down. The whole rule behind drumming is that you start off slow, and build it to whatever speed you want. It doesn't have to match the beat of the song, as long as you feel that you're with the drum and making music. When I drum I just get into the beat – it isn't a trance state, but I become very involved in the drumming.

The opening scene of Chinook Winds is a creation myth where you are drumming the play into existence out of the darkness.
For me, it was a chance to share my drumming with the audience and with my peers. Like you said, not too many people have seen Inuit drum. It's the whole mixture of drumming and dance at the same time.

Did you enjoy the experience of participating in Chinook Winds? Did it make a difference being part of a Native project?
It's been a lot of fun. I learned many different things. I went to my first powwow. I always feel at home with

other Inuit. I let myself be free. I don't hold anything back. From the very start I trust them. I can be myself around them without having to worry, Maybe I shouldn't say this, or maybe I shouldn't do this. And that's kind of what it's been like with this group. Sure, they're not Inuit, but they're still Native. I have that same feeling with them. I don't have to build walls around myself, like I would have to when I first went to high school in Winnipeg, Manitoba.

RIGHT: Jeff Tabvahtah in "Bear Dance." Photo Don Lee.
BELOW: Jeff Tabvahtah in "Residential School for Boys." Video still Richard Agecoutay.

Chinook Winds

Face Masking in Inuit Culture

Karla Jessen Williamson

Face Masking

The Inuit face masking as it was presented in Greenland was something that Christian missionaries shamed people from doing. Because of this, the tradition was facing oblivion. We were very lucky that a handful of Inuit of east Greenland kept the tradition alive until the 1950s and 1960s.

With the revitalization of the culture and language over the last few decades, a new generation of young Greenland artists have taken up the tradition, and ours is but one version of reinterpretation. I strongly relate the face masking to the Inuit understanding of equitable relationship between male and

Karla is Inuit, born in Greenland in 1954. She has attended school in Greenland, Denmark, and Canada. She has a Master's degree in Education, and has written on the Inuit relationship to the land and the implications of the education of Inuit children. She speaks Greenland Inuktitut, Danish, and English. She currently teaches at the University of Saskatchewan, specializing in cross-cultural education issues. Karla has given numerous lectures nationally and internationally, and is the editor of the *Journal of Indigenous Studies*. She is married and lives in Saskatoon with her husband and two children.

Photo Milton B. Taylor, Terry Jabusch (Imagery).

female human beings. At the same time the mask reveals our deep-seated under-standing and relationship with the rest of the living beings in this world.

The colour black signifies what we as human beings do not know about the surrounding universe. Inuit believe that the universe is where knowledge exists and is the home for the eternally existing creative forces. One of these creative forces is manifested as soul, in all living beings. Human beings have individual souls, which are individual names. Names and souls, being the same, carry human potential and could not arbitrarily become segmented through separate male and female entities. So, traditionally Inuit did not have genderized names.

The mask, then, has to show female and male characteristics on the masked face: a set of balls on the cheeks, accentuated by a mouth piece – originally a seal bone – to represent maleness in all of us.

Sylvia Ipirautaq Cloutier participates in an exploration of Inuit face-masking technique as part of the cultural workshops offered to the dancers during the *Chinook Winds* dance residency. Photo Monique Diabo-John.

The red colour signifies the femaleness (vulva) and can be on the forehead, or on the nose. The colour red evokes blood that, together with the white lines, represents the bones and life-lines of our ancestors and the bones of animals upon whom the Inuit depend for life.

Traditionally, the masking was performed when people least expected it, and real surprise is very much one of the key elements. Life in the far north is at times very unpredictable and sudden events may call for immediate evaluation and action to save lives. At an early age, youngsters are encouraged to face up to fear and to come to terms with it. Inability to overcome a sudden shock can have a devastating effect on community life.

Another important aspect of the face masking has to do with fertility. Like any group of people in the world, Inuit fear extinction and realize the importance of fertility to ensure the continuity of life on earth. The dances are typically performed with bent ankles and knees to imitate many animal movements. They include suggestive movements, at times explicit, and directed towards chosen targets for teasing.

ABOVE TOP: Siobhán Arnatsiaq-Murphy. *NEAR RIGHT:* Jeff Tabvahtah. Photos Don Lee. *OPPOSITE:* Jeff Tabvahtah in "Winds." Photo Heather Elton.

Chinook Winds

Northern Wind Song

Grandmother
I hear your wind song
enchant
drums echo
awakening ghost dancers
whose shadows
brush the red willow
mist forms
Dene-Deh
rise to your wind song
northern wind song
keeper
of the people
Grandmother
I lay my heart on the land
carry me home
beyond snow-blown dreams
to the tea dance
round fires dance round fires
with my ancestors
round fires dance round fires
to the beat of your
northern wind song
we become
keepers
of the land.

Morningstar Mercredi

ABOVE: Morningstar Mercredi is Dene from Fort Chipewyan, Alberta. She is a storyteller, actress, freelance model, playwright, and poet. This poem can be found in a collection of poetry from *The En'owkin Journal of First North American Peoples* entitled "Gatherings," Volume V, published by Theytus Books.

Tamara Podemski (foreground) reciting the poem "Northern Wind Song," while Sandra Laronde sings in Cree "Only She Is Beautiful," a song by the Red Bull Singers. This piece was called "Oka Female Warrior." Photo Don Lee.

Jerry P. Longboat

Jerry is a Cayuga/Mohawk from the Iroquois Confederacy, Six Nations of the Grand River, in Ontario, where he was born into the Turtle Clan. He was raised both on and off the reserve, and has sung and danced traditionally from an early age. Jerry received a B.F.A. degree specializing in Visual Arts from the University of Michigan. He has worked as a visual artist, graphic designer and, in theatre, as an actor, storyteller, and performance artist. He dances with the Karen Jamieson Dance Company in Vancouver, where he was in the original production of *Shattered Space* and the company's most recent production, *Stone Soup Project*, a collaborative process with the Git'Gisan people of northern British Columbia. Jerry recently completed a work study residency as an artist's services liaison for the Aboriginal Arts Program at The Banff Centre. Heather Elton interviewed Jerry Longboat about the difference between traditional and contemporary styles of dance, and the process of traditional Iroquois masking.

interview

ABOVE LEFT: Jerry Longboat (left) and Raoul Trujillo (right). Video stills Richard Agecoutay.

How do you make a traditional spiritual mask?

The process of making a traditional mask begins by centring and preparing yourself. It is a process of praying, making an offering, then communing and approaching the living tree from where the mask is birthed or carved. This is a process of actually carving the mask, removing it from the tree, and finishing it, and providing a welcoming feast for the mask.

And then does it have a specific purpose in a ceremony?

Yes. We were talking earlier about the use of traditional masks in contexts other than their original purpose, which I don't find appropriate at all. These masks were created out of specific needs of the community over time. They came for the spiritual well-being of the people. They have a specific life purpose that must be honoured as sacred. They came for the purpose of teaching us about balance and harmony, and they support us to moving through our fears. These original teachings must be respected from a traditional perspective and to distort this purpose in a contemporary context is disrespecting them.

Are traditional masks used only for spiritual ceremonies?

Those who own them and use them in a spiritual context use them spiritually at their discretion. The community knows who these people are and individuals go to them for spiritual assistance or healing. These healers have many years of experience with that process and have grown up with a relationship to that type of spiritual energy. It's very focused, clear, and strong.

Is that your path too?

Well, I envision it in my life. I have seen and experienced many things regarding traditional masks. When I was a young boy my parents were given a mask by my great-grandfather, who was a carver and mask-maker. This mask was part of our family. When I was about three or four, at specific times during the night I would be called by the mask. I would get up and go over to it and stand there and just look at it in the shadows. I remember it happening over and over again. I think that's where it started but I didn't realize this until I starting making masks in my early 20s. I've had many dreams with the false face in them.

Do you carve the masks you see in your dreams?

Sometimes. However, in terms of making a traditional mask there are specific types of faces and specific carving gestures in the wood that have been established over hundreds of years. These specific traditional shapes, forms, and types of expression create the integrity of the traditional mask. It is very important to stay in line with that when making a traditional mask and work towards revealing its true spirit.

Do you ever feel like a tool, as if the spirits are speaking through you?
Yes, very much. Ultimately, it's your connection with creative energy coming through and your internal gifts revealing themselves in different ways. The energy comes from the wood and through me; it mixes, and the mask emerges. It's born in those moments where the energies come together. Many times I approach mask-making with a design in mind, but I have to be open to let its own flow happen, and then the form comes forward. You need to take time to approach the mask, because it has its own spiritual journey to be fulfilled.

Do you dance with the mask?
I have begun to explore a little bit of that, although I have not danced in ceremony.

When you use a mask, do you go on a kind of journey?
It's very much like any kind of creation in that you surrender yourself to be a vessel for the energy coming through, you develop your abilities to respond to this wisdom, and so when you come together with the mask, and dance or move that mask (and that's what you're doing), you're trying to open a doorway for that life to come through and be expressed. Now, how that energy is directed has a lot to do with the mask and the role of the mask in the community. Ultimately, it's supposed to be shared. It's meant to serve that community. So, it's not for personal gain, although there are gifts there – when you surrender to the process it feeds you.

Are contemporary masks used as a vehicle for personal expression?
I use contemporary masks in that way to express a story or philosophy, or with teaching. My masks address the issues of today and the place we have come to as nations, and through that develop a contemporary language or contemporary form of expression, whether it be dance, theatre, or storytelling.

How did you start dancing?
We travelled on the powwow circuit when I was about seven or eight as an extended family and that's how it started. I stopped dancing in my mid-teens because I was heavily into competitive sports and doing the urban thing. I didn't come back to dance until I was 23.

Chinook Winds

Who taught you to dance and why do you dance Men's Traditional rather than Men's Fancy, or some other style?

Actually, Karen Pheasant reaffirmed a little bit of that journey for me. She said that it's very important to listen to your body, and as you begin to experiment with different forms of dance, you feel how your body moves and very naturally move into a type of dance whose rhythms and vibrations suit the expression of your body. Powwow dancing is about personal power and personal style and you express this to feed the nation.

Men's Traditional has a strong connection to the earth, the birds and animals, the old stories and traditional way of life. This is expressed in the movement and it works to develop openness and celebration of being human, connection to the community and brotherhood. For me, it's about exploring the original teachings of manhood so that I may understand myself and my responsibilities as I journey through life. This is where the outfit or regalia is so integral. It is an acknowledgement of my relationship to the winged creatures, to the four-legged and the wisdom they carry, even to the sense of colour and design to acknowledge balance, flow, and harmony in life.

You are an Iroquois, yet you are drawn to Men's Traditional Dance, which originates with Plains Indian culture. Why is that?

It's a Plains dance, but powwow is contemporary, and ultimately an expression of self, of the gifts that you possess, so 300 years ago the outfit that you would wear everyday would talk about your power.

It begins with the acknowledgement of the connection all Native people once shared. Throughout Turtle Island there were vast and extensive trade routes, and culture was shared before the coming of western influence and the division of North America. Powwow is a modern expression of those historic connections.

So, for me I have grown up integrating all these influences to serve my expression in movement, sound, and visual art. In my outfit you see evidence of Iroquois, or eastern woodland design, but also influences from elsewhere. I express what resonates with me. For example, I have a very strong connection with birds, so you'll see many parts of birds on my outfit. I've incorporated feathers on my shoulders and into some of the pieces I tie on to my outfit. My bustle is made of eagle feathers and I carry a raven staff. These teach us that life comes from the darkness and is born into the light. I believe this is a balanced view of creation.

Where do you get the birds?
Sometimes they are given to me, because people know that I make things to honour the power and gifts of the animals. Sometimes I find them.

Like roadkill?
For sure. I've done so much with hides and furs, using tails, bones, hooves, toes, and teeth. I make spiritual things like staffs, wing fans, rattles, and drums, all to support the continual process of life.

You've had experience both as a traditional dancer on the powwow circuit and as a contemporary dancer in a western theatre context. Is there a difference in the way you interact with the audience and how you feel as a performer?
Yes, very much. I come from a theatrical background and so I have come to know performance in terms of connecting with an audience and telling a story.

Contemporary dance is different because it mixes movement languages. It needs to be universal because you're telling a story to a whole range of people in the audience. When you dance at a powwow, the energy is specific and my expression originates from a different place than it does in the theatre.

Then there is the aspect of sound. The songs are there to direct the energy. I feel connected to the drum, to the earth, and to the animal energy around me.

When I'm in my outfit it is a strong manifestation of my personal power. I look very specific.

What makes a good traditional dancer?
I go to a powwow just to have the experience of dancing; not necessarily to win. I only average maybe five powwows a summer. So, I'm not totally committed. Some people do it full-time. It's their income. If I wanted to win, then I would need to make a full-time commitment and get known in the circuit.

But there are key technique elements within Men's Traditional Dance that judges look for, like ending precisely on the beat of the drum.
For sure. Smoothness and sensitivity are important. Interpretation and integration of the whole body is key. For Men's Traditional the judges look at how your head and shoulders move, the relationship of the hips to the legs and

Mask of "Waking Dream" by Jerry Longboat.
Photo Jerry Longboat.

feet. It is important that these elements are connected, moving with the drum, and full of personal style and integrity.

There's now a Men's Traditional Contemporary dance style that is a little bit more expressionistic. It shares dance steps with Men's Grass and Fancy Dance and has more flourishes. These traditional forms are changing.

During *Chinook Winds* you had the opportunity to interact with various Native communities in Alberta through feasts, sweats, and ceremonies. But, also within the group there were talking circles that created an atmosphere of trust and respect. The performance space was treated as a sacred space. Was the experience of working with an all-Native cast much different from working on other dance projects?

It can be, but when I work with the Karen Jamieson Dance Company we also have circles and do cultural sharing. So, she has a similar philosophy. We share how we feel. We check in. So there is a sense of that sacred space and that feeling of ensemble in circle. I work best that way, actually. Native people have grown up with extended families and communities, so we have that connection all our lives. When I come to that type of creative process I feel an immediate flow of energy. There is a strong connection in taking care, honouring, and respecting the ways

of the others in the group. That's how we are raised so it's very natural for us.

Chinook Winds seems unique in that it is a merging of traditional and contemporary forms of dance. And the Native performers come from many different cultural backgrounds. It must be difficult not to melt into a kind of pan-Indianism.

It's very challenging, probably more so for the choreographer than for the dancers. All the dancers come from various backgrounds in dance, so to bring them all together into an ensemble through training and rehearsal is a very challenging task. What makes it so special is that it's a dream that's happening; a vision that's unfolding. Alejandro Ronceria and Raoul Trujillo are the contemporaries in that they have carried on and nurtured the connection of dance and culture, not only to traditional dance. They're rooted in this time. They've learned traditional dance forms, but are passionate about telling contemporary stories. They recognize the need to train our own choreographers and writers. I think there's a real danger in other people appropriating our stories and telling us who we are. We've begun to awaken to the effects of this through the telling of history and we are reclaiming our truth in our own words, in our ceremonies, through our stories. Dance is a prolific part of this healing and self determination.

Native Youth
Culture Links
Rosa John

In the spring of 1996, during the symposium "For Tomorrow's Leaders We Gather Today," which was hosted by the Aboriginal Arts Program at The Banff Centre, community artists and educators spoke on the needs of our youth. We realized that the time has come to create a venue for urban Native youth so they have access to the many Aboriginal community organizations and individuals in the community.

Highlighted was the need for Native urban youth to link up with Aboriginal people who are successful in the arts and who use their art as a way of communicating their cultural identity. Culture and identity are two of the major steps towards healing and understanding the role of Native people on this Turtle Island. As a result of this symposium and other meetings like it, Kehewin Native Performance and Resource

Rosa has worked with youth for the past 15 years and is co-founder of Kehewin Native Performance. She graduates with an M.F.A. in Theatre Arts from the University of Calgary in 1998. Rosa was the cultural coordinator for *Chinook Winds*.

Rosa John at the symposium "For Tomorrow's Leaders We Gather Today," co-sponsored by the Aboriginal Arts Program, a partnership of the Aboriginal Film and Video Art Alliance and The Banff Centre for the Arts. Photo Sharon King.

Network, a non-profit performance and educational organization, created a program entitled *Culture Links. Culture Links '96* was a summer mentor project created to introduce urban Native youth to the Aboriginal arts community in Alberta. The project allowed the participants to visit mentors in the fields of museum curatorship, film and video, Native fashion design, and performance arts. A partnership was formed with several Aboriginal individuals and organizations, including the Aboriginal Dance Project at The Banff Centre. During the Native dance portion of *Culture Links '96*, we took the eight participants to Banff to visit artists in the Aboriginal Dance Project. We all slept in the spacious teepee that the Aboriginal Arts Program sometimes uses for its circles and meetings. The opportunity for these youth to stay in a teepee in the mountains is truly a gift for which we are grateful. The Aboriginal Dance Project provided a wonderful opportunity for the youth by inviting us to visit the rehearsals and talk with the participants over lunches and dinners. As well, we were given tickets so all the *Culture Links '96* youth could attend a performance of *Chinook Winds*.

During the two-day visit to Banff, the youth became aware of dance in relation to culture and history. It became not only a physical relationship with the dance, but a new voice. Dance had grown to become a new way of telling stories. They all wanted to dance! They wanted to explore the limits of their bodies and the infinite reach of movement and music. After only hours with the Aboriginal Dance Project participants, trust was established. There was no fear of how they might look, or what they might say. There was respect. They also knew that these participants were Native, just like them, and they watched as the dancers pushed themselves to heights that even they had no idea existed.

Just as humour is part of life and teaching within many Aboriginal societies, it had its place here. Even as Alejandro was teaching, the spirit of humour as teacher was prevalent. There was a time to concentrate on the movement, but he also recognized the need for laughter. For the *Culture Links '96* youth, this was of utmost importance. The person in power, the teacher/choreographer, whatever role he was to perform, Alejandro allowed himself to be seen as a human being. He was respected and awed simultaneously. The youth were able to experience the creation as a work-in-progress, as well as the tension, excitement, and anxiety of opening night. To have been part of this experience was exciting and filled me with hope for the future. At least these eight youth will have gained the knowledge and felt the presence of ancient cultures that are alive and well, flowing inside our veins. It is a presence that is impossible to ignore and can be called upon with a song, a feather, and a step.

Karen Pheasant

Karen Pheasant is an Ojibway band member of the Wikwemikong unceded reserve on Manitoulin Island, Ontario. She resides in the rural community of Wikwemikongsing with her three children. They have travelled extensively throughout Indian country on the powwow trail as Grass dancers and Jingle Dress dancers. Karen has been head dancer for the Toronto International SkyDome Powwow, and in 1992 she was invited to perform, along with her children, at the World Council for Indigenous People in Mexico City as part of the 500 Years celebration.

Karen is a committed proponent of education, having spearheaded *Path That We Walk,* a cultural program for Wikwemikong youth to encourage pride, knowledge, and confidence. Heather Elton interviewed Karen Pheasant about the history of the Jingle Dress Dance, dancing on the powwow circuit, and Karen's experience in *Chinook Winds.*

ABOVE: (left to right) Dawn Ireland-Noganosh, Alexandra Thomson, Siobhán Arnatsiaq-Murphy. Monique Diabo-John, Sylvia Ipirautaq Cloutier, Sandra Laronde in "Women's Traditional." Video still Michele L. *INSET:* Sandra Laronde in "Oka Female Warrior." Photo Don Lee.

interview

When did powwows first start in Ontario?

Dance celebrations have been around for centuries, but powwows are relatively recent. We just celebrated our 37th annual powwow in Wikwemikong (Manitoulin Island, Ontario). Many powwows are only 5 or 10 years old, but ours started in 1958. I was very fortunate that it was a part of my life. In a lot of communities it was something unheard of, yet they knew we had ours and everybody knew that powwows happened on the Plains.

I thought they were specific to Plains culture and didn't exist until recently in Ontario.

The Lake of the Woods people, near Kenora (Ontario), always had them. They just took them further back into the bush. I was about 8 years old when I made what I thought was an outfit. It was a piece of brown broadcloth with some fringe sewn on it, and I danced like that until my teens. When I was about 15 years old, I belonged to a youth group, and Millie Redman saw the desire in about a half a dozen of us girls, and she got some money together and some hides, and we made buckskin outfits. And at that time, we didn't know any better. Shawl Dancing is a relatively new style of

dance. In those days, Fancy Dance would have looked like contemporary Jingle Dress Dance does now. Thirty years ago, the footwork wasn't high. That's how I got started. I was wearing buckskin and doing Fancy Dance.

So why did you change to the Jingle Dress Dance?

I was in southern Alberta and still Shawl Dancing. I have these two uncles, John Mark from Morley (Alberta), he used to sing with Chiniki Lake drum, and Al Skead from Lake of the Woods. Within the same year John said, "Karen, you Ojibway people have a beautiful dress. How come you don't dance it?" And my uncle Al said, "You know we have a beautiful Ojibway dance, I don't know why you don't dance it." Later that same summer, I was dancing Jingle Dress.

When did you first see the Jingle Dress Dance?

Over 20 years ago, my mom took me to my first big powwow in Thunder Bay (Ontario). I remember seeing older women dance. I didn't know what it was at the time. They didn't have a category for them. They were dancing with these dresses. I didn't find out until many years later that it was Maggie White and the other families from the Lake of the Woods area. And that this is the dress that came to them through a dream.

Sometime when Maggie was a child, her father had this dream about the dress. There was illness in the family. They had offered their prayers and asked for help. The dream came to the old man for his daughter and then she was carried off wearing the dress. Maggie White passed away two years ago, at the age of 89. We always refer to her as the grandmother of Jingle Dresses.

So, the Jingle Dress Dance originates with the Ojibway people?

Yes, from the northern Lake of the Woods area. The dress was given to the people, and when I say "given," it means that dream was given to that family. Along with that came teachings and songs specifically for that dress. There are interpretations of those teachings. For instance, the 365 cones on a Jingle Dress remind us that each day we should offer prayers, and practice harmony and balance. I don't go into detail a lot because if there's someone that really wants to know, then they should make that visit to a grandma, or to an auntie.

And, there are some songs that come from the drum. The drum is sometimes referred to as the heartbeat of Mother Earth, of our people. The healing aspect is a combination of the song, the drum, the singers, the dress, the dancer, the women – all the women together.

Anytime that Jingle Dresses have been asked for a special healing song, they'll ask all the women to go. It's the power of many and unity. There's a proper way that we do the dance in the east, which I rarely see in the west.

When did the Jingle Dress Dance arrive out west?

One of my friends was just telling me when she and a bunch of women from the Whitefish Bay (Ontario) area came out here to share the dress. And when I was at Hobbema (Alberta), they announced it. They remembered when the dance first came there in 1981, when a group of them came. So the dress has been around for quite some time, but it came to this area then.

Were Copenhagen snuff cans used to make cones back east? Or, is that a western adaptation?

No, they used snuff can lids way back and it changed over to just tin lids. At one point, they were even wearing dew claws.

Are there contemporary songs specific to Jingle Dress Dance that are sung by drum groups at a powwow?

There are some songs that are composed just for Men's Traditional, just for Women's Fancy, just for Jingle Dress Dance. There are some straight songs like an Intertribal song, that we'll all dance to, but when I go to the middle of the floor and a song starts and I begin to dance, that's spiritually important for me. Dancing is my healing.

So, an old song or a contemporary one, whether it's designed for the Jingle Dress Dance or an Intertribal, can be equally as powerful. It's really about the spirit of the song and your connection with it.

Yeah. We were dancing in Atlanta for the Olympics, doing performances a few times a day. About the second week, it seemed like the drum group were just doing the song and I was just doing the dance steps. At the end of that show, I felt awful. I realized that if all I did was execute the movement, then I'm not a dancer. So the following day I decided not to do that. No matter what. If the song doesn't touch me then I'll go way within myself to seek that passion. When I dance I'm not just executing

movement, I'm dancing with passion. So that's what I mean when I say it doesn't have to be a traditional or contemporary song. They have to be sung with heart.

How did you teach the Jingle Dress Dance to the dancers at Banff?

I came to Banff thinking that I was going to be teaching just the history of the Jingle Dress Dance and there's a lot of teachings and stories to tell before the dance. So what happened is we needed to get into teaching the steps. And like I said, when you start just doing the steps you're not doing the dance. I was sharing and telling Alejandro this but he said, "Tomorrow, you're going to go right into steps." He's the director, so of course I did. I switched gears and started to do that. I told them "one, two, one, two" or whatever, but the company wasn't picking it up. It must be something to do with western dance training as opposed to Indigenous dance. They were dancing with no centre, no energy. They were trying to execute steps, like what I ended up doing in Atlanta when I got so discouraged. When you talk to any strong powwow dancer who dances full-time, that's not footwork, it's their spirit dancing.

I was telling the women, "Know your centre, this is where the song comes into your body." I was saying, "Listen to the drum," and they were listening, but they were still not catching the rhythm of the drum, the heartbeat. It was literally going in their ear and they were waiting for it to get to their feet. I was thinking, How am I going to explain about understanding that drum? So, I started to work with the chakras and energy systems, and talking about the heart and the song going through their back, and telling them to hear that song. I touched their back, behind their heart, and when the drum came they could feel it. The look on the girls' faces when we did it that way was amazing.

While I understand the importance of the connection to spirit, there still is a specific Jingle Dress Dance step that makes it look different from the Shawl Dance. Each style of dance has its basic footwork, but some dancers are able to develop their own style.

Can you describe the essential footwork for the Jingle Dress Dance? The original Jingle Dress Dance that the old grandmas danced was very low to the ground with one foot going in front of the other, much like a Charleston. That's the straight dance and then there's the

side step, which is like the Round Dance. Contemporary style is higher off the ground with some footwork, more body movement, and more fan movement. Old style Jingle Dress Dance has no fan. All styles of dance sometimes borrow from other styles.

For instance, the Shawl outfits never had yokes or capes on them. All you wore was a shawl. Then, sometime in the late 70s, these capes started to appear with beaded big collars at first, then they got bigger. Now, some are halfway down your back.

The evolution of dance forms in the powwow context is interesting. The older forms that have been around since the beginning, like the Grass Dance or Men's Traditional, have become more contemporary. The word "powwow" is an eastern word that means a gathering. Traditionally, Plains people would move entire camps, their families, their extended families, and go and visit. And this is the whole idea of where powwow started. The men would storytell and there would be songs to go with that. So now, do we say this is a ceremony? Do we say this is a social? What it was, they were visiting and they were an oral-based society. And so we sang and we danced. The women weren't within the dance circle.

This was explained to me once by Evelyn Eaglespeaker, who comes from the Blood reserve, we were discussing how in Ojibway tradition women don't sit at the drum, but with the Blackfoot, women can sit at the drum, and I was telling her I was in a conflict about it. She said, "You know, Karen, times change and if we were going by strict tradition women wouldn't even be dancing." We didn't even have a place in that circle. We were just getting the hides, cooking, and taking care of the kids, while men were hunting and telling hunting stories, singing hunting songs. But times have changed and women started dancing.

First, we were allowed on the outside of the circle; that was a stationary dance. Soon, we were doing the Walk Dance. Then, this whole idea of Men's Fancy emerged with the two bustles. In 1800s, during *The Wild West Show*, white people wanted more colour and more flash, so the Men's Traditional turned into Men's Fancy with more colours and two bustles, instead of the one bustle, with almost acrobatic movements. Of course, the women, not wanting to be left out of anything, started too. The women put on the men's bustles and danced the men's dance.

You've travelled throughout North America on the powwow circuit. Are powwows in Florida any different than powwows in Alberta?

Powwows across North America tend to be staffed by northern people, with northern drums. And the neat thing about it is that in February I'll be standing amongst palm trees in Florida with the same people I'm usually dancing with in the summer – Blackstone, Black Lodge, the MCs, the arena directors, and the head judges. They're all from the north. I went to a powwow outside of L.A. and Chiniki Lake, from Morley (Alberta), was host drum. The culture of powwow is so exciting, so vibrant.

Are Seminole dance styles included in a Florida powwow?

In a separate venue, much like a festival. Just because a woman is dancing Jingle Dress, it's not safe to assume that she's an Ojibway woman.

So it's like a travelling show with the same people and the same dances?

There are many types of powwows. There's your rez powwow and there are urban powwows. There are contest powwows like those in Albuquerque

(New Mexico), Oklahoma City (Oklahoma), Toronto SkyDome (Ontario), Winnipeg Jets Arena (Manitoba), and the Big Four here in Calgary (Alberta), to name a few, which showcase the best of the best. These dancers have all worked hard, have many outfits and dance full-time. And they're competing for top dollars.

So there's one particular powwow at the Jets arena in Winnipeg. It's the final day and only the top 10 finalists were dancing. So we're talking serious competition. And what they do for the top 10 is spotlight them. The organizers said, "We have true artists here, we have true performers. And we should treat them that way. They should be with spotlights and all the grandeur."

And, I was sitting with a traditional Jingle Dress dancer who mostly just dances at traditional powwows. She said "Gee, Karen, I don't know about the spotlight dancing, and top 10 finalists, and drum roll, and all of this. What happened to the tradition of why we have dance?" And I said, "Well, I think what happened is the world is recognizing Native dance as an art form, as much as ballet, jazz, or any other dance form. It's to be recognized, appreciated, and shown to the world, with as much pride and dignity as any other western dance form. And so, this is a venue for that. This is a venue for professional artists who dance full-time.

I met a young dancer at Gleichen (Alberta) who told me he learned to dance from watching videos of other dancers. He copies their movement, gets the basic steps down, and then enhances it with his own style.

We have words about that kind of stuff. I was visiting with Reggie Black Plume. He's 68 years old and from the Blood reserve. Now, we were sitting together at the Ermineskin powwow and one thing I really notice about powwows in Alberta is the amount of contemporary movement in Native dance. So we got talking about that and he said, "I've been dancing since 1938, and back then it didn't matter what we wore, what was important was your style of dance and hearing that song. Now all you see is a bunch of Christmas trees out there." And that says it all about that young dancer you met.

What do you look for when judging a champion dancer?

Their individual style. The completeness of their outfit. Their timing and interpretation to the drum.

What are your thoughts about *Chinook Winds* and the fusion of modern and traditional styles of Native dance?

It's awesome. It's high time that our art form is appreciated, like ballet and jazz. Native dance companies have existed for years. When I was 15, I saw a Western Plains dance tour perform at Ontario Place in Toronto (Ontario). Those have been going on for years. My family has been doing dance presentations for quite a few years. We went to Mexico City and shared with the Indigenous Celebration '94, and New Zealand. And then there's been Native theatre productions with some kind of Native dance in it.

And as a dancer, whenever I went to those performances I always wondered, Gee, they're Native people, how come they've never consulted with actual dancers on the dance part? It seemed like the Native dance part of theatre wasn't authentic, wasn't researched. Yet dancers are abundant. Every province has a number of high-calibre dancers. There are enough of us dancers who make it

our life to know our dance, and we always wonder why we're not asked for advice.

So when I was invited to Banff, I was really honoured and excited that I was being asked. It's really neat that the company has found Native dancers.

LEFT: "Women's Traditional." Video still Michele L.
BELOW: The Reverend Evelyn White Eye, of Walpole Island First Nation, at Six Nations Powwow. Photo Jerry Longboat.

Siobhán Arnatsiaq-Murphy

Siobhán is of Inuit/Irish descent. Born in Iqaluit, Nunavut, she has returned home after many years of living in Ottawa. While in Ottawa she was involved in the International Inuit Youth Exchange Program. She lived in Chile for three months with the Mapuche Indians. On returning to Canada, Siobhán participated in the Inuit Fashion Show at the Museum of Civilization in Hull, Québec, in February 1996. As a child Siobhán was involved in dance classes and this return to dance has sprung from a desire to speak for and about her culture and herself.

Dance has played an integral part in my life and in my society. I was taught to dance for strength, pain, healing, joy and, most of all, celebration. Through the expression of dance, especially in Aboriginal cultures, a step into the past may be retained, explored, revived, or created. In an Aboriginal culture our identity is found in our dance. I have danced in many ceremonies and sang to the Creator. Dance has always been an emotional journey where I can find my spiritual self.

Photo Richard Agecoutay.

Sylvia Ipirautaq Cloutier

Sylvia is an Inuk from Nunavik (Northern Québec). She speaks English and French, and is working to regain her Inuit language and culture. She has always loved the world of music and dance. Although a tragic car accident kept her from dancing for some years, she is returning to dance in a very powerful way. Sylvia holds the dream of bringing Aboriginal dance back to her community as a creative alternative to combat the social and cultural challenges they presently face.

I speak from my heart when I say that I love to dance. This beautiful art is like a language to me. The freedom of expression and movement is a gift given to me by the Creator that I can share with others. When I speak with my body it is deeper than words at times. As a child I remember dance as a collection of sweet memories that ended in tragedy. Today, the journey continues on a different path. It is the beat of the drum that carries me to what I believe in: my Inuit culture. When I dance I'm in a different world, somewhere special where I can be myself. It's on stage where I become alive.

Photo Richard Agecoutay.

Monique Diabo-John

Monique is of Mohawk-Tiano descent. She will be graduating from high school this year in Calgary. She plans to continue her education at university. She began Fancy Dancing at an early age, then moved to the traditional Jingle Dress at the age of 13, which she continues to dance today. Monique has performed with the Kehewin Native Performance and Resource Network for six years. She performed in a music video for the group Indian Nation and *On the Outside* with Ground Zero Theatre Productions. She is a graduate of the Four Winds Theatre Camp. She co-wrote a performance piece about AIDS, performed at the Pedagogy of the Oppressed Conference with Augusto Boal and Paul Freire. She is a committee member for the United Way and has travelled extensively.

I am interested in creating change for my generation. I think that if we can educate non-Native people and show Native people that we know who we are through our dances, maybe we can see a positive change in the future. I am interested in working with people from different nations.

Photo Richard Agecoutay.

Jonathan Fisher

Jonathan is an Ojibway/Odawa from the Wikwemikong unceded reserve on Manitoulin Island, Ontario. His recent theatre credits include *Toronto at Dreamers Rock* (Theatre Direct), *No Totem for My Story*, *Diva Ojibway* (Native Earth Performing Arts), and N. Scott Momaday's play *The Indolent Boys* (Syracuse Stage). Some film and television credits include *The Oath*, *Law of the Jungle*, and the award-winning short film *City of Dreams*. Jonathan co-wrote the screenplay *Redskin, Grey Bar Hotel* for Nepantla Films. Most recently he performed a piece from his play *Dances with Goldust*, co-written with George Chiang, for the Going for Broke Festival. Jonathan would like to dedicate this performance to the memory of Merrance Trudeau.

Gaining knowledge from the Aboriginal Dance Project and learning more about the process of dance will not only help develop my craft as an actor but will also be a useful tool for myself if I ever feel the need to branch out into my own "physical-based" works somewhere down the road. This is a direction I feel passionate about pursuing.

Video still Richard Agecoutay.

Dawn Ireland-Noganosh

Dawn is Oneida and is currently a member of the Chippewas of Rama First Nation near Barrie, Ontario. She has worked as the publishing coordinator for *Aboriginal Voices*, a Native American arts magazine, and has recently coordinated an anthology of Aboriginal women's writings entitled *Into the Moon* published by the Association for Native Development in the Performing and Visual Arts in collaboration with Sister Vision Press. Dawn recently completed a contract with the Aboriginal Music Project as program coordinator. She is the coordinator of the Couchiching Drum and Dance Troup in Rama, Ontario, and has been dancing traditionally for the past seven years.

Dancing has been a form of healing for me. When I'm dancing I internalize the rhythm and it becomes a part of me. My mind, body, and spirit are all in synch and it's just me and the drum.

Sandra Laronde

Sandra is Anishinabe, originally from Temagami, Ontario, and resides in Toronto. She is a performer, writer, and a founder of Native Women in the Arts. Sandra was last seen in *Ravens* (Native Earth Performing Arts). Other credits include *The Manitoulin Incident* (De-ba-je-mu-jig Theatre), *Mercy Quilt* (CBC Radio Drama), and *Turtle Fell from the Sky*. Sandra is very pleased to have worked with the people in the project and extends many thanks to the Aboriginal Film and Video Art Alliance and the Aboriginal Arts Program at The Banff Centre for the Arts.

Physical movement is the life-throb of ages dancing in my blood at this very moment. Though many of us have suffered great losses, our bodies continue to carry rich cultural memory, image life, knowledge, emotion, and spirit. Within our very bodies is a vast ocean of deep ancestral memory, and to dance this ebb and flow is to respond to the creative nature granted to us in this world of life. The generation of women, within myself and yet to come, conjure unspoken words and songs. In a vast dreaming dance inside our Grandmother's red womb.
All my relations

Photo Richard Agecoutay.

Photo Monica McKenna.

Chinook Winds

Jerry P. Longboat

Jerry is Cayuga/Mohawk from the Iroquois
Confederacy, Six Nations of the Grand River
and is a member of the Turtle Clan. Jerry
has extensive training in theatre as an
actor, performer, and storyteller. He has sung
and danced traditionally from an early age.
He recently performed with the Karen
Jamieson Dance Company in the original
piece *Shattered Space*. Prior to this he was
involved as a dancer in the collaborative
creative process of Karen's *Stone Soup Project*
with the Git'Gisan people of northern British
Columbia.

*Throughout my work as a performer, I have
found that the most profound source of
inspiration has been the body itself; the very
thing that roots me here in this life. As such it
has been taught to me by my elders that
when we are born of our bodies we become a
hereditary recipient of all the wisdom of our
ancestors who had lived before us ... in
essence a vast body of experience and
memory. With this I have come to understand
the truest expression of a culture is in its
dances and songs; the body never lies. Let us
be bold and tell all.*

Tamara Ceshia Podemski

Born to Saulteaux-Israeli parents, Tamara
currently lives in Toronto. Encouraged by her
father and two sisters, she graduated from
the Claude Watson Performing Arts School,
where she studied theatre, opera, ballet,
modern, jazz, tap, folk, Latin, and ballroom
dance during the 10-year program. Tamara
has performed nationally and internationally.
She danced for the opening of the 1994
Aboriginal Achievement Awards. Her acting
credits include the feature film *Dance Me
Outside* (CBC), *The Rez*, *Blue Hawk*, and *Ready
or Not*. She has the lead in an upcoming film,
Chalk, due out in 1998. Tamara has been
Fancy Dancing since she was seven years old.

*I have much faith in the Aboriginal Dance
Project because it covers so much ground on
the essential aspects of dance: history,
tradition, and culture. These elements are as
profitable as the actual technical training.
The intellectual, spiritual, and emotional
enrichment from this program will enhance me
as an individual, a student, a dancer and will
increase my chances of contributing to the
international community of dance.*

Photo Helen Tansi.

Daniel J. Secord

Daniel is a traditional dancer from the Mississaugas of the New Credit First Nation in southern Ontario. Daniel is of Ojibway, Mohawk, and Scottish descent. He is presently a member of the Kanata Native Dance Theatre of Six Nations and has recently returned from a three-month tour in Asia. *Chinook Winds* has been Daniel's first experience with contemporary dance, one he finds an exciting challenge. Upon his return home, Daniel will travel to northern Ontario to research and learn social dances of the Ojibway nation, as a training program for Kanata Native Dance Theatre.

The more I learn about dance the more I can take back to my people – Native dance and traditions as well as contemporary ideas in dance. This will help me professionally but more importantly, I want to bring these ideas and dances to my people and community to rekindle our traditions and inspire others to dance and participate in our social traditions. The children of our nations need to be shown the proper ways of dancing.

Photo Richard Agecoutay.

Jeff Tabvahtah

Jeff Tabvahtah is from Arviat, Nunavut. He comes from a traditional community where drum dancing and other activities were introduced to him at a young age. Jeff began to drum at 15. Since then, he's learned different kinds of drumming and dancing, as well as how to make a drum through his great-uncle. Jeff appeared in *Qaggiq '95 and '96*, an Inuit fashion show at the Museum of Civilization in Hull, Québec. He has also appeared in the film *Trial at Fortitude Bay* in 1994.

Dance is an expression of emotion shared with the audience. Without verbal communication, the audience can listen and interpret the feeling of the dance piece, whether it's classical, modern, or traditional. In our traditional dance we are able to share a piece of our history, our culture, our stories. For me when I dance, there is a deep feeling of pride.

Video still Richard Agecoutay.

Chinook Winds

Allan Blake Tailfeathers

Allan's major experience has been in contemporary dance, performing with Studio One in Lethbridge, Alberta. More recently he has become fascinated with the potential of combining contemporary technique with traditional Grass Dance forms.

Ever since I was young, I have always experienced Native dancing. When I was old enough I asked my parents if I could dance. My mom gathered together my uncle's old powwow dance outfit and I began to dance powwow. I learned from watching others and asking friends to show me. When I dance I feel a part of my culture, it gives me a sense of identity. It always makes me proud of my heritage, knowing that I have the chance to carry it on for upcoming generations.

Photo Richard Agecoutay.

Alexandra Thomson

Alex was last in Banff for the Aboriginal Theatre Ensemble in the winter of 1995. Recent work includes *Percy's Edge* for the Festival of Native and Métis Plays at 25th St. Theatre, a Globe Theatre tour of *Sitting on Paradise,* and *The Duchess* for Alberta Theatre Projects playRites Festival. She is a graduate of the Centre for Indigenous Theatre and George Brown Theatre School. She is co-founder with a group of women of the Ahaso Med'sin So & Company, an Aboriginal theatre company based in Saskatoon. She is currently researching the story of her grandfather Malcom Norris for the writing of a new play.

I am reminded of the old people of our culture who still dance. I feel that I can contribute with spirit and focus what I can no longer do with athletic feats. The Aboriginal Dance Project is an opportunity to learn, to make discoveries, to take risks, and to step further on the path. I hope to come away with new inspiration and ideas to share with my community.

Video still Richard Agecoutay.

Acknowledgements

Chi meegwetch to the Aboriginal Film and Video Art Alliance, who negotiated a cultural partnership with The Banff Centre for the Arts, enabling Aboriginal artists to have a strong presence here, to work collectively within a cultural context. *Hi hi* to the Alliance Artists, Advisory and Council: Alanis Obomsawin, Maria Campbell, Bernelda Wheeler, Doreen Jensen, Loretta Todd, Marjorie Beaucage, Jeanette Armstrong, Sadie Buck, Wil Campbell, Don Fiddler, Denis Lacroix, and Joane Cardinal-Schubert.

Also *hi hi* to Carol Phillips, Director of The Banff Centre for the Arts, who has been unswerving in her support of Aboriginal artists and the practice of self governance in the arts – always affirming our right to tell our stories in our own way.

Meegwetch to Don Stein, Director of Writing and Publishing at The Banff Centre for the Arts, who supported *Chinook Winds* from the beginning.

A special thanks to those who dreamed this project, and all who worked on this book, including those who gave their time for the interviews, and those who wrote their stories.

Marrie Mumford

Image Credits

Back cover and pages 24–25 inspired by a Plains War Bonnet motif. Inside front cover, page facing dedication, and page 87 inspired by a Cheyenne Woman's Dress c. 1880. Page facing title page, title page, and contents page inspired by a Winnebago Star Dream design. Page 52 inspired by a Haida Grizzly Bear totem pole from Tanu, British Columbia.